D0926997

# American Mosaic

# American Mosaic

## AFRICAN-AMERICAN CONTRIBUTIONS
# The History of the Blues

Sandy Asirvatham

CHELSEA HOUSE
PUBLISHERS
A Haights Cross Communications Company

Philadelphia

*Frontis:* Bluesman John Lee Hooker was born in Mississippi and eventually made his way to Detroit to start his career. His best-known compositions are "Boom Boom Boom," "Crawling King Snake" and "Boogie Chillen." He eventually enjoyed a renaissance in the 1990s with help from such artists as Bonnie Raitt, Ry Cooder and Keith Richards.

## CHELSEA HOUSE PUBLISHERS

VP, New Product Development   Sally Cheney
Director of Production   Kim Shinners
Creative Manager   Takeshi Takahashi
Manufacturing Manager   Diann Grasse

## Staff for THE HISTORY OF THE BLUES

Associate Editor   Benjamin Xavier Kim
Production Editor   Jaimie Winkler
Picture Researcher   Pat Holl
Cover and Series Designer   Keith Trego
Layout   21st Century Publishing and Communications, Inc.

A Haights Cross Communications ✦ Company
http://www.chelseahouse.com

First Printing

1  3  5  7  9  8  6  4  2

Library of Congress Cataloging-in-Publication Data

Asirvatham, Sandy.
  The history of blues / by Sandhya Asirvatham.
    p. cm.—(American mosaic)
Includes index.
Summary: A comprehensive look at the history of blues music, from its origins to the present time, including the musicians involved in creating that history.
  ISBN 0-7910-7266-5 (hardcover)—ISBN 0-7910-7490-0 (paperback)
  1. Blues (Music)—History and criticism—Juvenile literature.
[1. Blues (Music)—History and criticism.] I. Title. II. Series.
ML3521.A85 2003
781.643'09—dc21
                                    2002154035

# Table of Contents

Legendary blues guitarist Buddy Guy is one of the many musicians carrying on the blues tradition and bringing the music to appreciative crowds all over the world. This uniquely American form of music is performed with a variety of instruments, from full electric bands to a single slide guitar.

# From African to African-American

The music we call the blues is deeply and broadly ingrained in the American experience. It doesn't matter whether you know what name to call the sound when you hear it; it doesn't matter if you couldn't identify a single blues artist by name. It makes no difference if you are a fan of hip-hop, grunge, or opera. Nor does it matter what part of this country you live in or what kind of music your local radio stations play. If you have a television, or ever go the movies, or have traveled even just a little bit, chances are that you have been exposed to the sound of the blues: the plaintive wailing of a guitar; the tense yet poignant sound of a singer sliding between pitches; perhaps even the slow, steady driving rhythm of a drummer marking or implying an insistent stream of triplets.

The blues have become an international music, played in a variety of old and new styles, by men and women of all races and nationalities. But the blues are a specifically American invention, born of the historical trauma that shaped this nation in its infancy. Without the capture and enslavement of millions of African people by the European settlers of this continent, the blues would never have existed. And without the blues, it's hard to imagine the existence of any of its musical offspring and close cousins: rock, jazz, hip-hop, soul, funk, gospel, disco, Motown. Almost all indigenous American popular music, as well as Caribbean and South American styles—calypso, reggae, salsa—have some connection, either with blues music itself, or with the larger cultural implications of the encounter between black Africans and white Europeans in the New World. As scholar Mary Ellison puts it in her study *Extensions of the Blues*:

> The blues are a living tradition that imparts a sense of historical identity to those who create musical extensions of the blues. The blues tradition has had a shaping influence on almost all the popular music to emerge from America. It had been called "the fundamental American music. It is the tough, hard, durable stuff that all our styles and genres have in common." It is not only the rhythms but also the experience of compassion of the blues that flow out in a somewhat diluted way into ballads, country and western, rock, and soul.

Even country music, which is considered the cultural provenance of Southern whites, owes a large debt to black music. Ellison quotes country music writer Bill Malone, who said:

> Nowhere is the peculiar love-hate relationship that has prevailed among the southern races more evidenced than in country music. Country music—seemingly the must "pure white" of all American musical forms—has borrowed heavily from the Negro. White Southerners who would be horrified at the idea of mixing socially with Negroes have enthusiastically accepted

their musical offerings: the spirituals, the blues, ragtime, jazz, and a variety of instrumental techniques. In our own era the Negro rhythms of rhythm and blues, rock and roll, and folk rock have captivated southern youth whose parents in some cases may be Ku Klux Klan and Citizens' Council members [i.e., radical segregationists]. It has never been possible in this country to segregate musical forms.

Although its roots stretch back into the centuries and its specific origins are more than a little murky, the style we recognize as blues music is relatively young—a hundred and twenty years or so. While the earliest blues musicians have long since left us, a few of the developers of the modern blues sound—B. B. King, for example—are still alive and actively performing. Meanwhile, a younger generation of American artists—Keb'Mo, Robben Ford, Susan Tedeschi, and many others—continues to mine the blues heritage to create personal sounds that are fresh and new but respectful of the tradition.

For a musical tradition to become "universal" in the way that blues has, however, it must have grown pretty far removed from the circumstances that gave it birth. Through a process of commercialization—which began as early as 1920, with Mamie Smith's best-selling recording of "Crazy Blues"—the blues was transformed. What was once the spontaneous, organic expression of a very particular culture eventually turned into a self-conscious musical "style" to be performed, broadcast, imitated, and reinvented countless times.

The original blues served very deep spiritual and emotional needs of the communities and the individuals that developed it. It was a "functional" music that could not be separated from all other aspects of life: work and money, love and sex, family and friendship—and even worship. Although all forms of music once had a firm and explicit connection with religion, this interrelationship was retained much more clearly in African-American culture than in the dominant European-based culture of mainstream America.

The blues has been called "devil's music" and has been noted for its use of secular themes—particularly, for its overt and often humorous sexual references. But in connecting blues music to its African roots, knowledgeable historians have illuminated the essential seriousness of this music. In this way, the blues is revealed to be not merely a musical "style"—and certainly not merely a fashion or fad dreamed up by trend-chasing record executives—but a meaningful response to the tragedies and absurdities of life as experienced by a dislocated, traumatized, and powerless group of people.

Although the institution of slavery has appeared in various forms and in different places throughout human history, slavery in the United States was distinguished by its near-universal racial component: black African slaves and white European masters. In most previous slave societies, slaves and masters were often of closely related tribes or similar ethnic groups. Early English colonists in the seventeenth century made heavy use of white indentured servants—poor Europeans who traded four to seven years of their labor in exchange for passage to the New World—as well as captured Native American slaves. Toward the end of the seventeenth century, as economic conditions improved in Europe, fewer people were willing to sell themselves into servitude. At the same time, the colonial economy was rapidly growing and landowners were desperate to meet their labor shortage. This circumstance, coupled with the increasing strength and power of the English navy, put the colonists in the position to dominate the transatlantic slave trade and bring millions of Africans across the ocean.

Slavery was not unknown in Africa before Europeans arrived. Among the tribes of coastal West Africa, where most of America's slaves eventually came from, it was a common practice. In a

The slave trade brought Africans over to the New World, placing them in a new and strange land and infusing their lives with a sense of displacement. The experience would ultimately help spur the development of blues music.

broad area known as Senegambia (now the nations of Senegal and Gambia), a once-powerful empire splintered off during the sixteenth century into warring city-states. For tumultuous decades, these bellicose factions regularly sold their prisoners-of-war into slavery. Eventually, Islamic rulers from North Africa and seafaring Europeans began purchasing slaves from Senegambian warlords who, according to writer Robert Palmer, "had prospered in war and owned more slaves than they could profitably use." Historian Melville Hersovits has also noted that in the West African kingdom of Dahomey, "a kind of plantation system was found under which an absentee ownership, with the ruler as principal, demanded the utmost return from the estates, and thus created conditions of labor resembling the regime the slaves were to encounter in the New World."

But the transportation of so many Africans to a completely foreign land was a new kind of trauma. "When black people got to this country, they were Africans, a foreign people," wrote Imamu Amiri Baraka (formerly known as Amiri Baraka and as LeRoi Jones) in his classic 1963 treatise *Blues People*. "Their customs, attitudes, desires, were shaped to a different place, a radically different life." African slaves, Baraka wrote, had been brought "to a country, a culture, a society, that was, and is, in terms of purely philosophical correlatives, the complete antithesis of [their] own version of man's life on earth." In Baraka's view, the mere fact of enslavement was not as cruel as the fact of this extreme cultural and philosophical dislocation.

Colonial America, as Baraka puts it, was "the largest single repository for *humanism* in the New World. It witnessed the complete emergence of secular man. The Church and religion had become only a part of man's life. They were no longer, as in the pre-Renaissance Western World, the one reason for man's existence." African cultures, in contrast, retained a diametrically opposed view of the world, in which religion was inseparable from all other aspects of daily life. This African worldview was pressured, challenged, transformed, and yet—as we shall see— in some sense retained among the slaves of the early colonies and among their children and grandchildren.

In keeping with the overall structure of secular European society, music and all other arts had been separated from religious life. As Baraka explains, "before the Renaissance, art could find its way into the lives of almost all the people because all art issued from the Church, and the Church was at the very center of Western man's life. But the discarding of the religious attitude for the 'enlightened' concepts of the Renaissance also created the schism between what was art and what was life." In contrast, "it was, and is, inconceivable in the African culture to make a separation between music, dancing, song . . . and a man's life or his worship of his gods. *Expression* issued from life, and *was* beauty."

The African view that life itself is completely infused with music, song, and worship is still much in evidence today. In his recent book *Black Music of Two Worlds: African, Caribbean, Latin, and African-American Traditions*, the author and record producer John Storm Roberts notes that:

Traditional African music differs from European music in that it tends to be more directly tied to function. Up to a point, all music anywhere has a function: to accompany worship or courtship; to make work go better; or simply to give pleasure. Yet there is no doubt that in Africa it is more closely bound up with the details of daily living than in Europe. There is an immense amount of music for special purposes. All continents have lullabies for putting babies to sleep, of course, but in the Fon area of Dahomey (now Benin) there is a song children learn to sing on the loss of their first tooth. The Akin of Ghana have a song of derision aimed at habitual bed wetters sung at a special ritual designed to cure enuresis. Punishment for wrongdoing frequently has its own music: the Akin have special drums, played to accompany a petty thief while he is paraded through town with whatever he stole in his hands; and the Bagman of Cameroun have some eerie and impressive music to be played when a court official is taken to be hanged.

Moreover, Roberts explains, music is a crucial element in African religious practice. "Whereas it is not essential to Christian rituals—however much it may add to their impressiveness— many African ceremonies simply could not take place at all without the appropriate music." This, most observers have noted, is as true today as it was 400 years ago.

Thus we can begin to see what a tragically disruptive thing happened when African people were taken from their native land and forced into punishing labor in a harsh new atmosphere, where they were no longer able to practice the religious and social rituals that gave their lives structure and meaning. Our current term "culture shock" can barely begin to describe what a terrible, gut-wrenching sense of alienation, confusion, and fear these people must have experienced.

Yet even slavery could not destroy the fundamental human impulse to make sense of life through stories, songs, and rituals. Perhaps the extremity of the circumstance even helped strengthen that impulse. In responding to the bewildering new hardships of their captivity, African slaves took their memories of their original culture, mixed them with observations about their new—and, to say the least, unexpected circumstances—and ultimately create new ideas and forms. These new ideas and forms were neither wholly African nor wholly European, but something else entirely: African-American.

Toiling in American fields, slaves brought from Africa would have sung "pure" African chants and work songs. As Baraka speculates, "Most West Africans were farmers and, I am certain, these agricultural farm songs could have been used in the fields of the New World in the same manner as the Old.

But the lyrics of a song that said, 'After the planting, if the gods bring rain,/ My family, my ancestors, be rich as they are beautiful,' could not apply in the dreadful circumstances of slavery." Gradually, then, the specifically African references would have to change; and eventually, the songs sung by the first slaves' children and grandchildren, born on non-African soil, would more accurately reflect their particular time, place, and lot in life.

West African tribesmen used drums to communicate across distances and to summon each other to ritualistic "secret meeting"—a tradition that lived on in the New World, in the form of "camp meetings" among plantation slaves. Fearing slave revolts or escapes, slave owners eventually banned the use of drums among their African captives.

# 2

# Traditions in the New World

The original African cultures of the U.S. slave population were predominantly oral rather than literate. In the seventeenth century, Africans from the Senegambia region recorded their history not in writing but through song and dance—another aspect in which music served a profoundly "functional" role. Each tribe had professional singers and storytellers (called *griots*) who served as the comprehensive living libraries of tribal history and helped pass important myths and customs down through the generations. As music critic and historian Peter O. E. Bekker Jr., explains in his book *The Story of the Blues*, "Every event of consequence—births, deaths, hunts, feasts, plantings, harvests—was celebrated in song, in which the entire tribe would very often participate . . . [W]hole villages would take part in elaborate rituals involving call-and-response singing; frenzied, complex drumming; and complicated hand-clapping."

Another related tradition, the "secret meeting"—a ritual in which tribal elders took younger members to an isolated place to pass on certain important customs—survived passage to the New World and became "camp meetings" in the colonies. Plantation slaves would summon each other to remote areas, often using drums to communicate in much the way their ancestors had done. Unlike their European-descended captors and owners, who were cultured to think of the drum as a purely percussive instrument, West African people had developed a very sophisticated language using different drum pitches to imitate the inflections, and ultimately the meanings, of spoken words. This was particularly possible in West Africa because the spoken languages of these peoples were (and still are) "pitch-tone" languages, in which a single syllable or word can have different meanings based on whether the speaker is using a high-, middle-, or low-level pitch.

Once called by drum or other signal to these secret meetings, Bekker writes, the slaves "danced and sang, often at fever pitch, for many hours. It was common for them to rage bitterly against their bondage and plan ways of escape (the goal was usually to go back to Africa). The 'minutes' of these meetings often emerged as a communal song that could be heard for weeks afterward, plaintively drifting through the slave quarters."

Not surprisingly, slave owners imposed bans on such meetings, and in many places, began outlawing the use of drums and other African instruments. Although this undoubtedly resulted in the end of some aspects of the culture the Africans brought with them from their native continent, these bans and laws did *not* spell the end of the culture as a whole. As Baraka observes in *Blues People*,

> where the use of the African drum was strictly forbidden, other percussive devices had to be found, like the empty oil drums that led to the development of the West Indian steel bands. Or the metal wash basin turned upside down and floated in another basin that sounds, when beaten, like an African hollow-log drum. The Negro's way in this part of the Western world was adaptation and reinterpretation. The banjo (an African word) is an African instrument,

and the xylophone, used now in all Western concert orchestras, was also brought over by the Africans. But the survival of the *system* of African music is much more significant than the existence of a few isolated and finally superfluous features.

Out of the oppressed and embattled musical culture of Africans on American soil, one of the hardiest surviving forms was the *work song*. Work songs were, and still are, a ubiquitous feature of life in Africa, particularly in regions that require a great deal of communal rather than individual labor. For example, work songs are far less common among tribes who live in rainforest regions—where crop-harvesting is often a solitary pursuit—than among those who live and work in the open fields of savanna regions. In general, though, the idea that singing makes work more bearable is a fundamentally African attitude. As John Storm Roberts writes in *Black Music of the Two Worlds*, "The heyday of the collective work song in the United States was the period of slavery, and not only because more people were nearer to their African background. Another reason was the nature of plantation work, which was frequently team work."

While slave owners may have feared and banned other forms of communal music-making among slaves—after all, it was during a "secret meeting" that the slave Nat Turner was able to plan and execute his rebellion in 1831 in Virginia, which took over 70 lives—they were all too happy to encourage their laborers to sing while they worked. According to Professor Eileen Southern in her book *The Music of Black Americans: A History*, ex-slave and abolitionist writer Frederick Douglass reported that

A silent slave is not liked by masters or overseers. "*Make a noise*" and "*bear a hand*," are the words usually addressed to the slaves when there is silence amongst them. This may account for the almost constant singing heard in the southern states. There was, generally, more or less singing among the teamsters, as it was one means of letting the overseer know where they were, and that they were moving on with the work.

While husking corn, slaves might sing:

> Hoo-ray, hoo-ray, ho! Roun' de corn, Sal-ly!
> Hoo-ray for all de lub-ly la-dies! Roun' de corn, Sal-ly!

While cutting wood, slaves might be paired off on opposite sides of a tree, both of them singing to keep the tempo of their axe-blows steady:

> A cold frosty morning,
> The niggers feeling good,
> Take your ax upon your shoulder,
> Nigger, talk to the wood.

Songs like these were crucial to help large groups of slaves maintain the rhythm of their coordinated movements. Southern notes that a song collector wrote in 1868:

> Long ago, when the mowing-machine and reaper were as yet unthought of, it was not uncommon to see, in a Kentucky harvest-field, fifteen or twenty "cradlers" swinging their brawny arms in unison as they cut the ripened grain, and moving with the regulated cadence of the leader's song. The scene repeated the poet's picture of ancient oarsmen and the chanter seated high above the rowers, keeping time with staff and voice . . . For such a song strong emphasis of rhythm was, of course, more important than words.

The slave owners and plantation overseers who encouraged communal work-singing were doing so for a very practical reason that had nothing to do with "culture," of course. They were concerned with maintaining the pace and orderliness of their workers, in order to uphold the productivity and profitability of their fields. In so many other ways, the colonists of pre-revolutionary America, and later the slaveholding citizens of both Southern and Northern states, sought to diminish and destroy their slaves' cultural and familial bonds. The law did not recognize

The slave Nat Turner planned and executed a slave rebellion at a "secret meeting" in Virginia in 1831. Although musical instruments such as drums had been banned for fear of allowing slaves opportunities to meet and unite in dissent, the slaves were still encouraged to sing while they worked.

family connections among slaves; husbands, wives, children, or grandparents were sold off and separated from one another without regard to ties of blood and love. Traditional African gods and religious practices were generally prohibited; in some parts of the South, according to Baraka, "'conjuring' or the use of 'hoodoo' or 'devil talk' was punishable by death or, at the very least, whipping."

It was a form of divide-and-conquer: by tearing them apart from most of the cultural and familial links that bonded them, slave owners effectively tried to dehumanize their slaves, thus making them more controllable as chattel or "property." Yet paradoxically, the retention of work songs may have served to create a strong sense of community among slaves who had little else to cling to. In his 1995 book *Keeping Together in Time: Dance and Drill in Human History*, the military historian William H. McNeill investigated the fact that when a group of human beings does any kind of steady rhythmic motion together—be it a military drill, a religious song and dance, a parade down a city street, or a calisthenics routine on a factory floor—it creates a powerful sense of well-being and togetherness among its individual members. Indeed, participation in these kinds of collective rituals can even induce a trance-state, a "generalized emotional exaltation." So although secret meetings and explicit religious rituals were forbidden, the underlying spirit and function of those music-infused African tribal gatherings may have lived on among the slave population through work songs.

Even after the importation of new slaves from Africa was outlawed in 1808, the number of slaves in the United States continued to grow through birth—and while slavery in the Northern states shrunk until it was nearly nonexistent, the institution itself grew with the western expansion of the country and the emigration of slaveholding families from the southern seaboard states to Midwest and western regions. From the turn of the century to the dawn of the Civil War in the 1860s, the U.S. slave population grew from about 1.2 million to almost 4 million. These slaves were entirely African-American—they had all been born into captivity on this soil. Yet, as we shall see, they retained certain cultural connections with their African roots—primarily through music.

As Baraka observed, "iron-working, wood-carving, weaving, etc., died out quickly in the United States. Almost every material aspect of African culture took a new less obvious form or was wiped out altogether . . . Music, dance, religion, do not have *artifacts* as their end products, so they were saved. These non-material aspects of the African's culture were almost impossible to eradicate. And these are the most apparent legacies of the African past, even to the contemporary black American."

Throughout the early colonial period, most white Americans had absolutely no philosophical problem with the institution of slavery. Having come from the highly stratified societies of Europe, where the upper classes brutally exploited the labor of the poor, these colonists had no reason to question the slave-master power hierarchy. Their children and grandchildren began to believe more firmly in the natural equality of all human beings—although whites were still generally considered superior to blacks—and as a result, slaves were generally treated more humanely in the period just before the Civil War. The Northern states, whose economies had never been quite as dependent on slave labor as those of the South, began to abolish slavery and establish laws by which even children of slaves could become free by a certain age. But in the Southern states and western territories, the ultimate end of slavery only came about as a result of several coalescing factors or events: an increasingly vocal national abolition movement; broad social, economic, and political upheavals that resulted in the terribly bloody and traumatizing Civil War (1861-1884); and two legal precedents, the Emancipation Proclamation, issued by President Abraham Lincoln in 1863, and the Thirteenth Amendment to the Constitution, ratified in late 1865.

In the last quarter of the nineteenth century, slavery was officially over—but for Americans of African desent, there were still many more struggles ahead.

A statue entitled "The Freed Slave" was shown in Memorial Hall at the 1876 Centennial Exposition in Philadelphia. After the Civil War, many freed slaves migrated to other parts of the country, while those who remained in the South often worked as fieldhands, moving from one plantation to another to find work.

# 3

# Down in
# the Delta

**A**fter the Civil War, this country was a shambles in many
ways. In particular, the agrarian economy of the South was
shattered. Although freed from bondage by law, black Americans
experienced harsh and new kinds of hardships. Struggling to reunite
a bitterly divided nation, the national government made attempts to
ensure the rights and freedoms of African-American citizens, even if
it meant having to occupy certain southern and western territories
using federal military troops. For a brief time, it seemed as if
many of the promises of emancipation—including the rights to
vote for and hold public office, access to free public education, the
elimination of discriminatory laws—would be kept. But in the
decades following the war, as powerful members of the former
Confederacy began to regain their authority in local and state
politics, they found ways to erode or eliminate the newly established
rights of blacks. The landmark came in 1896 with the Supreme

Court's decision in *Plessy v. Ferguson*—the case that officially sanctioned the "Jim Crow" laws of segregation and the "separate-but-equal" caste system in most Southern states.

While some blacks began what would eventually become a mass migration to Northern cities in search of a more equitable society, those who remained in the South and West often ended up staying on plantations that had been abandoned or sold by their owners. Those owners, whose wealth in the form of slaves had been obliterated by the emancipation, were in some cases almost as destitute as their former slaves. What evolved in this vacuum of mirror-image misery was the sharecropper system. As Bekker describes the system in *The Story of the Blues*,

> Blacks who agreed to stay on plantations to sow, pick, and chop cotton were promised a share of the proceeds at harvest time. The system worked well on paper, but in practice many blacks never seemed to make out. In some cases, because planters deducted the cost of food, clothing, and housing from an already meager wage, the sharecropper would end the year in debt. The debt would be carried over to the next year, and the next, until the sharecropper was again living in servitude, this time virtual if not actual.

Of course, as Bekker notes, because sharecroppers were not actually slaves by law, there was nothing to prevent them from abandoning the plantation and leaving debts behind. In the rich, fertile lands of the Mississippi Delta—former swamplands that became the epicenter of the nation's cotton production— it was not unusual for field hands to move from one plantation to another, following jobs from here to there but also "reveling in the freedom of travel for its own sake—a heady experience for a former slave."

Some of these traveling men were musicians, and some of them undoubtedly played music that was the precursor of the blues. But no one knows the exact origins of the music we now recognize as "Delta blues." In *Deep Blues*, his detailed account of the music, writer Robert Palmer begins his discussion by noting that "black American music as it was sung and played in the rural South was both a continuation of deep and tenacious African traditions and a creative response to a brutal, desperate situation." By the time of the sharecroppers, African-American musical expression had grown to encompass a broad spectrum of possibilities, from the sounds of "pure" African religious music to the styles of European classical music. Wrote Palmer, "And while one would expect to find field workers whose parents were born in African playing more African music and blacks whose forebears had been house servants for generations playing in a more acculturated [European-based] style, this was not always the case. Black musicians . . . have always been pragmatic. There must have been a number of musicians who . . . could play anything from African whooping music to folk ballads to fiddle and banjo breakdowns to the latest Tin Pan Alley hits, as required."

Even before the Civil War, there had been professional black musicians who worked in plantation bands, playing white classical and dance music and possibly some early forms of syncopated proto-jazz. Emancipation killed off the plantation groups but also made it possible for black instrumentalists—fiddlers, banjo players, mandolin players, and others—to take to the roads. In the decades after the Civil War, black "songsters" or "musicianers" traveled the countryside and played a repertoire that mixed elements of white country music—for example, narrative ballads that originated from Scotland or England—with African-American styles. Palmer believes that "even though many white and black *songs* were similar or the same, black performing style, with its grainy vocal textures and emphasis on rhythmic momentum, remained distinctive. And gradually the songsters developed a body of music that diverged more and more radically from the interracial common stock."

It wasn't a songster, however, who gave the term "the blues" its popular usage. William Christopher Handy, known as W. C. Handy (1873-1958), was a formally trained musician who played the cornet (a kind of early trumpet) and was a band-leader for minstrel shows throughout the South. Minstrelsy was originally a form of entertainment that whites developed based on caricatures—often of a rather cruel and degrading nature—of black people. Minstrel shows became so popular that even black actors began dressing in "blackface" to do such song-and-dance routines. Both white and black minstrel shows made use of black musicians as accompanists, and it was in this environment that W. C. Handy first plied his trade. An Alabama native, Handy later ran one of the most successful black dance orchestras in the Delta. Operating out of Clarksdale and traveling extensively throughout the South, this band specialized in ragtime, cakewalks, and other dances, as well as light classical music played from written scores. Some of these tunes were called "blues"—such as Handy's composition "East St. Louis Blues"—and helped influence a separate strain of music, known as "classic blues" or "urban blues," which was sung primarily by women backed by jazz musicians. But ultimately these separate styles had only a little in common with the guitar-based music eventually known as Delta blues.

In 1903, Handy was waiting for a train that was nine hours late. He fell asleep on a bench in the Clarksdale station, but was awoken by the sound he later called "the weirdest music I had ever heard." Palmer recreates the scene as follows:

> [A] black man in ragged clothes sat down beside [Handy] and began playing a guitar, pressing a knife against the strings to get a slurred, moaning, voicelike sound that closely followed his singing. Handy woke up to this music, and the first words he heard the man sing were "Goin' where the Southern cross the Dog." The line was repeated three times, answered in each case by the slide guitar. Politely, Handy asked what it meant, and the guitarist rolled his eyes mirthfully. In Moorehead, farther south

Minstrel bandleader W. C. (William Christopher) Handy is known as "the Father of the Blues," although he was its earliest popularizer, not its inventor. Handy first heard the haunting sound of the blues at a train station, where he met a man who played guitar by sliding a knife across its strings.

near the Sunflower River in the heart of the Delta, the tracks of the Yazoo & Mississippi Valley Railroad, known to the locals as the Yellow Dog, crossed the tracks of the Southern at right angles. The man was on his way to Moorehead, and he was singing about it.

Handy, a formally trained musician, had never been overly impressed by the black folk music tradition of the songsters. He went on record to say that he thought of field hollers and work songs as "primitive music." But this guitarist's playing intrigued him. It had nothing in common with the usual steady, regular strumming of typical black folk-song accompaniments, nor did it make use of the elaborate picking style of ragtime guitar. Instead, the haunting quality of the slide against the guitar strings created a second "voice," a human-like response to the singer's words.

There had once been a certain kind of African one-stringed instrument that employed this form of sliding. But by the end of the nineteenth century, only children ever engaged in this rudimentary form of music by fashioning one-stringed instruments out of scraps of wood and wire. The slide guitar that Handy heard was a real innovation. Other musicians recalled hearing the slide guitar technique for the first time around 1900. It had nothing to do with the jigs, reels, and other well-established forms of dance tunes played by professional traveling musicians such as Handy. And yet, in the space of a few decades, this kind of slide guitar would become ubiquitous, creating a sound forever associated with the notion of "blues music."

Listening to the music long after its inception, experts have been able to identify numerous ingredients that went into making the sound—field hollers, songster ballads, church music, and African percussion music. But to this day, we have no real knowledge of where the sound of the blues was first conceived and born, no way to pinpoint where that guitarist making "weird music" at the Clarksdale station first learned to play it. Nor is entirely clear how "the blues" got its name, although we know that the phrase "having the blues" was an old slang expression, derived from Elizabethan England, that whites and blacks both used to describe a state of melancholy or depression.

Yet we do have a pretty good idea of where the Delta blues—the music that would most directly influence later electric blues and rock 'n' roll—spent its infancy and early childhood: a cotton plantation of forty square miles in Sunflower County, Mississippi.

A typical gathering at the end of the day in the cotton fields involving music and dancing. Early bluesman Charley Patton would travel throughout the Delta playing music for such events and working in the cottonfields only when he had to.

# 4

# Dockery's Plantation and Beyond

Will Dockery was, in many ways, a typical white Southern landowner of the time. His forefathers on both sides of the family had been wealthy slaveholders before the Civil War, but at the end of the nineteenth century they were now almost penniless. With a loan from an uncle in the cotton business, Dockery launched an effort to regain the family fortune by founding a forty-square-mile plantation near the town of Cleveland, Mississippi, in 1895.

He and his family worked hard to clear the malaria-infested swamplands and take advantage of that nutrient-rich bottomland for the planting of cotton. Dockery later began hiring blacks to work his plantation for about fifty cents a day, the average amount paid by white landowners in that area. It was hard money earned through hard labor, but for many black Mississippians, it was the best available option. Palmer writes,

[E]ven the lowest daily wage was better than trying to eke out a living farming rocky ground or working on a small white-owned farm for room and board. And the system that prevailed in the Delta was flexible enough to offer a variety of options. You could work by the day and be ready to move on at any time, you could work your way up to a more remunerative position, you could enter into one of a number of possible sharecropping arrangements. As blacks from southern Mississippi began drifting north, they found that Will Dockery wasn't interested in tricking them out of their wages or otherwise mistreating them, unlike some other white men, and they told their friends.

The sounds that came to be known as "the blues" seem to have developed in several different places at around the same time—including Memphis, Tennessee, parts of Texas, and the Carolina Piedmont region. Each region produced its own unique "flavor" of the blues. But by far the greatest number of influential blues innovators—the ones who continued to influence several later generations of musicians—came from the Mississippi Delta. And in fact, most of these original country bluesmen ended up having some connection with the Dockery plantation, a phenomenally successful agricultural business which came to dominate the region and which was still a working plantation as late as the 1970s.

One of the earliest of these men was Charley Patton. Patton was born somewhere around 1885, one of the eleven children of Bill and Anne Patton. The Pattons were all workers on Will Dockery's cotton plantation. Charley—whose light, wavy hair, yellow skin, and Caucasian features caused people to whisper that he may have actually been the son of a white man—was enlisted early on to be a field hand and mule driver on the plantation. But Charley's true vocation was music, and he pursued it vigorously, despite his father's belief that playing nonreligious music for parties was a sin. Even Bill Patton's frequent whippings couldn't keep Charley from his music.

In his teens, Charley learned the guitar and began working music jobs for both black and white audiences, often as a member of the local Chatmon family band. The Chatmons, like most musicians of the day, played ballads, ragtime tunes, minstrel and Tin Pan Alley show tunes, white dance music such as jigs and reels, and Negro spirituals. Charley learned all these musical styles and more, but then began developing his own individual flavor of music. He sang his songs in a deep, gruff voice—a surprising feature for such a physically small man—and accompanied himself with a rough, gritty guitar style that later musicians would emulate.

Some historians say that in his years with the Chatmons, Charley also spent time learning from a man named Henry Sloan, a cotton picker whose life story is even less well known than Patton's. Sloan may have been the first true blues guitarist whose name we know: he was probably the one who showed Charley how to pick single notes to create a vocal-sounding melodic line, rather than strumming chords and thumping on the body of the guitar in the manner of the day. Sloan may also have been the one to introduce Charley to the use of a bottleneck or knife blade to create the "slide guitar" sound. Without these techniques, Patton may have remained just another minstrel, beloved at the time but mostly forgotten by later musicians and fans.

As a young man and throughout his life, Charley Patton loved to have a good time. He drank, caroused, and used his musical skills to charm women. His onstage antics became legendary: like the blues and rock guitarists who came after him, Charley "amused audiences by holding his guitar behind his back, on his head, or upside down on his shoulders, for instance, plunking out contorted solo parts while dancing around," according to Bekker. After being fired as a work hand at Dockery's when he was still in his late teens, he traveled throughout the Delta, making music, taking farm jobs only when it was absolutely necessary, and otherwise living off the generosity of his girlfriends. Even for a professional musician who could avoid the fields, the black

Southern man's life was a hard one, filled with the humiliations and privations of being a second-class citizen in a white-dominant culture. Palmer writes that Patton

> adapted to it well enough despite his lingering rage, which he tended to take out on his women, sometimes by beating them with a handy guitar. He suffered his dark moods . . . but he also had fun, or something like it. He rarely worked for whites except to furnish a night's entertainment, and he was never tied to a menial job or a plot of land for very long. He went where he pleased, stayed as long as he pleased, stayed as intoxicated as he pleased, left when he wanted to, and had his pick of the women wherever he went.

Even though he was no longer living under the roof or watchful eye of his disapproving father, Charley clearly felt some ambivalence about his lifestyle: he would alternate long periods of drunkenness with temporary "conversions" to a godly way of life. Palmer describes his flip-flopping morality:

> Throughout his life he would periodically repent, renounce loose women and alcohol, and take to studying his Bible in preparation for a preaching career. Once, when he was still a young man, he volunteered to preach in a little country church, and although he ran out the back door in a blind panic after coming face to face with the congregation, he later managed to deliver a number of successful sermons. But his conversions never lasted very long. An old friend would show up with a guitar and news of a house party or a big picnic a few miles down the road, and Charley would bottle up and go.

Many later bluesmen would experience similar struggles between their worldly musical ambitions and the godly lifestyle advocated by their kinfolk. Later in his life, Charley Patton would record a large collection of religious songs as well as his influential blues tunes. As Bekker asserts, "There is really no irony in that;

Picking cotton was just about the only employment option for black Mississippians at the turn of the century. Many young, transient bluesmen eked out a living by working the cotton plantations in the day, performing music at night, and traveling all across the Delta in search of both kinds of employment.

these spirituals and hymns were among the first songs he learned on the plantation, and they stayed with him throughout his life. He performed the material in the same gruff and sometimes mongrel way as he performed the blues, often using a bottleneck or knife blade as a guitar slide."

Although party-loving bluesmen may have had trouble reconciling their "sinful" lifestyles with their earnest spiritual yearnings, today's scholars see a profound connection between blues music and the general religious beliefs of turn-of-the-century

African-American culture. Bluesmen like Henry Sloan, Charley Patton, and their students and disciples used their musical gifts to entertain crowds and charm female fans, but the music itself can be seen to serve a deeper "functional" role, reminiscent of African music's functionality. Religious historian James H. Cone considers blues music to be closely related to "slave seculars," songs that expressed African-American slaves' skepticism of Christianity as it was preached to them by whites. A hymn with the lyrics "Reign, Master Jesus, reign," might be parodied as follows: "Rain Masser, rain hard! Rain flour and lard, and a big hog head, Down in my back yard!"

These songs weren't anti-spiritual or atheistic, Cone explains, but they did reflect the difficulty black people had when attempting to relate Christian concepts to their oppressed situation. The blues played a similar role—Cone writes that "they invited black people to embrace the reality and truth of black experience." Rather than reject God, Cone says, the blues ignore God by embracing the joys and sorrows of life on earth. So a man like Charley Patton would sing, for example, about the hardships of romance, a topic he knew all too well. (In this tune, we can see that the stereotypical structure of the blues song—either three identical or nearly identical lines, or two identical lines with a third "response" line—had already appeared by Patton's time; the exact origin of this format is not known.)

> Yes, you know it you know it, you know you done me wrong
> Yes, you know it you know it, you know you done done me wrong
> Yes, you know it you know it, you know you done done me wrong
>
> Yes, I cried last night and I ain't gonna cry no more
> Yes, I cried last night and I ain't gonna cry no more
> But the good book tells us you got to reap just what you sow

By the time Patton was in his late teens or early twenties, Will Dockery had built his plantation into an agricultural empire—

huge plots of land stretching from Mississippi to Arkansas and linked together by roads and railroad tracks. Along this vast terrain, more and more young men with guitars in tow could be found traveling by foot or rail in search of a party to play, a short-term job in the fields, or a warm bed for the night. By the first two decades of the new century, Charley's teacher Henry Sloan joined the growing numbers of blacks migrating north to Chicago in search of better-paying work and a better life. But Charley Patton remained in the vicinity of Dockery's and became the most celebrated bluesman in the region, a widely popular Saturday-night entertainer, and a mentor to talented younger musicians.

Singer Mamie Smith's 1920 recording of "Crazy Blues" was an instant bestseller. Its phenomenal popularity among black album-buyers prompted record companies to flood the market with dozens of female blues singers—some of them truly talented, others merely in the right place at the right time.

# 5

# Ladies Who Hollered

Around the same time that Charley Patton and other bluesmen were developing their signature sound, black female singers in the Northern cities were on the cusp of their golden era. In the late 1910s, record executives were just beginning to figure out that there was money to be made by catering to the musical tastes of black Americans. In 1920 in New York, a singer named Mamie Smith recorded four record "sides" all written by a seasoned black songwriter named Perry Bradford. "Crazy Blues," one of the four Bradford songs that Smith recorded, became so popular that it started a nationwide craze for female blues singers and helped launch the market for so-called "race records" specifically aimed at African-American listeners.

The time was an auspicious one for African-American culture in general. In a neighborhood in New York City known as Harlem, writers such as Alain Locke, Jean Toomer, and Zora Neale Hurston were publishing innovative works of fiction or philosophy, read mostly by a growing population of educated, culturally sophisticated African Americans in the urban North. In the late 1910s and early 1920s, the elegant, superbly executed military music of James Reese Europe and his Army Band helped inspire a new level in race-consciousness and racial pride among blacks, and demonstrated to skeptical white Americans and Europeans that African Americans were wholly capable of playing—and excelling at—formal concert music.

A different but parallel energy in rural areas first fueled the market for the folksy, gritty, yet expertly accomplished songs of the blues queens, typically backed by stylish instrumental jazz combos—a style that came to be known as "classic blues." Mamie Smith and Perry Bradford were both veterans of the black vaude-ville entertainment circuit, a series of clubs, theaters, tent-shows, and other venues around the nation that had catered to rural black audiences since the beginning of the twentieth century. The most powerful single source of African-American entertainment was known as TOBA, the Theatre Owners' Booking Agency (or, as embittered, underpaid performers sometimes called it, "Tough On Black Artists"). TOBA had developed nearly seventy venues where folks could see black singers, dancing girls, comedians, magicians, snake charmers, or jazz bands.

Live performances by beloved musicians whetted the public's appetite for recordings they could play at home at their leisure. But for a long time, white-owned recording companies were reluc-tant to enter this arena. According to Daphne Duvall Harrison, author of *Black Pearls: Blues Queens of the 1920s*, most white promoters underestimated both the talent and the potential marketability of black artists. She writes, "Many hours were spent by Perry Bradford and W. C. Handy trying to convince the record companies that black women blues singers had a ready market of black consumers who wanted to buy their recordings." Managers of these companies continued to claim that black women's voices were too gruff, their diction too unschooled, or their songs unsuitable for the mass market.

But Perry Bradford, in particular, was extremely persistent—Harrison calls him a "hustler." Eager to achieve his own fame as a composer, Bradford pounded miles of pavement and knocked on plenty of doors before finally finding an amenable studio: the Okeh division of General Phonograph. Okeh's first releases were two Bradford tunes sung by Mamie Smith: "This Thing Called Love" and "You Can't Keep a Good Man Down." In March 1920, prompted by almost no promotional efforts of marketing, black Americans purchased every single copy of this disc—which had a pressing of approximately 100,000—in a matter of weeks and months. Okeh soon rushed to produce the "Crazy Blues" disc and also published the sheet music for the song, both of which sold in record numbers and started a new boom. Within a year, the so-called "race market" was flooded with blues singers one after the other, each one with a promotional tag-line, and each one promising to be the "best yet" by the record companies.

After Mamie Smith came Mary Stafford ("First Colored Girl to Sing for Columbia"), Ethel Waters ("Sweet Mama Stringbean"), Lucille Hegamin ("The Cameo Girl"), Alberta Hunter ("Prima Donna of Blues Singers"), and dozens of others. Some of these classic blueswomen were true musical giants destined for long-term fame and historical recognition, while others were devoid of talent—or luck.

Born in 1895, Alberta Hunter became a star in Europe and is credited with introducing the blues to the European continent. She sang in a London production of the musical *Show Boat* along with the great African-American concert artist Paul Robeson; went through a twenty-year period after World War II when she trained as a nurse and worked in a New York hospital; and finally enjoyed a revival of her singing career from age 81 until her death in 1977. Victoria "Queen" Spivey (1906-1976) sang in blues clubs and in churches from her teens until the time of her death, and established her own recording company in the 1960s. Like Hunter, Beulah "Sippie" Wallace (1896-1986) spent a long period out of the limelight but returned to blues singing in her old age.

In her history *The Music of Black Americans*, Eileen Southern says these women's voices "ranged from lilting soprano to deep contralto, from expressive, soulful wails to abrasive, gut-bucket groans and moans. Since most of the women were vaudeville artists, their singing inevitably reflected a sophisticated approach to the song material." Singing in clubs, cabarets, theaters, or recording studios, these women offered music that, although blues-influenced, often had much in common with ballads, Tin Pan Alley standards, and vaudeville songs. Traveling nationally or sometimes internationally, they also led lives considerably different from the country bluesmen who had not yet been discovered by the mainstream music industry.

The oldest of the great blues queens was Gertrude "Ma" Rainey, born in 1886 in Columbus, Georgia, who was probably the first singer to use blues as a part of a minstrel repertoire. With her deep, earthy, contralto voice and straightforward, narrative singing style, Ma Rainey attracted hordes of followers through her Southern tent shows. In 1923, after Rainey had been performing for nearly 25 years, Paramount Records recorded her songs and marketed her as the "Mother of the Blues," and she became a national star.

A natural talent who consistently earned the respect of her backing musicians despite her lack of formal training, Rainey was also a born star. According to Harrison, Ma Rainey was a vivacious woman who loved glittery jewels, heavily beaded dresses, and shiny headbands. Her publicity photos display a broad, winning smile enhanced with sparkling gold caps. She sang songs that helped define the thematic territory of female blues singers—songs of love, sex, infidelity, revenge, loneliness, poverty, and hard work. But Rainey also had a flair for comedy, and an ability to see the humor in everyday troubles. In *Those Dogs of Mine*, for example, Rainey sang mournfully about the aching corns on her feet.

Eight years younger than Ma Rainey, Bessie Smith, who was known as the "Empress of the Blues," became the most famous and influential of all the female blues singers of this period.

Gertrude "Ma" Rainey, one of the earliest blues singers, had been performing for nearly twenty-five years in tent shows around the South before Paramount Records recorded her songs and marketed her as "The Mother of the Blues."

When she was still in her teens she was touring with the same troupe that featured Ma Rainey, and by age twenty she was headed toward stardom. Like Rainey, she had a performance manner and singing style that combined the grittiness of down-home country blues with the sophisticated polish of urban jazz and blues. In 1923, her debut recordings—"Down Home Blues" and "Gulf Coast Blues"—sold one million copies in their first year. Harrison writes of her impact on the music scene:

> By the time her career ended during the Depression her records had sold an estimated six to ten million copies. Jazz musicians, gospel singers, and popular song vocalists all acknowledge Bessie as a major influence because of her keen sense of timing, her expressiveness, and her flawless phrasing . . . She drained each phrase of its substance and bathed each tone with warmth, anger, or pathos. But above all, her naturally fine voice and her uncanny ability to transform any material into a great performance earned her a superb reputation . . . Her association with jazz musicians had a mutually beneficial effect and she developed vocal techniques as sophisticated as the techniques used by a horn player.

Bessie Smith ultimately wrote or co-wrote many of the songs that made her famous, such as "Nobody Knows You When You're Down And Out" and "Empty Bed Blues." At the height of her fame, she was the highest paid black performer in the world, commanding $2,000 a week. She was still famous when the Great Depression hit in 1929 and caused the bottom to fall out of the music market, but like so many performers, she found herself struggling to make ends meet. She died when she was thirty-nine in a car crash near Clarksville, Mississippi, in 1937.

Women like Rainey and Smith sang songs that expressed the particular difficulties of being a black woman, but with a level of expressiveness that made those experiences understandable to many kinds of people. Despite the melancholy nature of the blues, these songs often inspired laughter—sometimes a raunchy and good-natured kind of laughter, sometimes a more rueful response to life's absurdities and heartaches. Clever, colorful language was the best way to get one's point across. So, for example, a blueswomen wouldn't just call her unfaithful boyfriend a cheat or a hound dog; instead, according to Harrison, she'd sing, "Your love is like a radio, you are broadcasting everywhere."

In these songs, along with humor and cleverness, there was also a great deal of plainspoken pain, frustration, and disaffection. The narrator of a typical Bessie Smith tune might lament over a lost love:

Settin' in the house with ev'rything on my mind
Settin' in the house with ev'rything on my mind
Lookin' at the clock an' can't even tell the time

Walkin' to my window, and lookin' out of my door
Walkin' to my window, and lookin' out of my door
Wishin' that my man would come home once more

But the blueswoman—or rather, the character she portrayed in song—wasn't always a victim of life's vicissitudes; defiant and proud, she knew she had a hand in her own troubles, at times:

You can send me up the river or send me to that mean ole jail
You can send me up the river or send me to that mean ole jail
I killed my man and I don't need no bail

Yet Bessie and the others were not afraid to express moments of hope, as well:

It's a long old road, but I'm gonna find the end,
It's a long old road, but I'm gonna find the end.
And when I get back I'm gonna shake hands with a friend.

As entertaining and moving as this music could be for both its practitioners and its listeners, however, did it also serve a deeper function among African Americans? Harrison seems to think so:

The blues . . . are a means of articulating experience and demonstrating a toughness of spirit by creating and re-creating that experience. . . . Fluency in language is considered a powerful tool for establishing and maintaining status in the black community. Thus a man or woman who has mastered the art of signifying, rapping, or orating can subdue any challenger without striking a blow and is held in high esteem.

In this analysis, singing the blues was a way for the singer to gain power and status through articulating his or her experiences—but it was also a way of reinforcing the audience's sense of identity as members of the black community. Harrison writes that the blues are "paradoxical in that they contain the expression of the agony and pain of life as experienced by blacks in America"; yet the blues help release that pain and renew the spirit, for both the singer and the listeners. According to Harrison, a blues pianist named Roosevelt Sykes once memorably put it, "Blues is like a doctor. A blues player . . . plays for the worried people . . . See, they enjoy it. Like the doctor works from the outside of the body to the inside of the body. But the blues works on the insides of the inside."

By some accounts, however, the broad appeal of the 1920s blues queens helped change the fundamental nature of the music. As Amiri Baraka notes in *Blues People*, the classic urban blues of the 1920s was

> the first Negro music that appeared in a formal context as enter-
> tainment, though it still contained the harsh, uncompromising
> reality of the earlier [rural] blues forms. It was, in effect, the perfect
> balance between the two worlds, and as such, it represented a
> clearly definable step by the Negro back into the mainstream of
> American society. Primitive blues [e.g., the kind Charley Patton
> and other Delta musicians would have played] had been almost a
> conscious expression of the Negro's individuality and equally
> important, his separateness . . . Classic blues attempts a universality
> that earlier blues forms could not even envision.

For an art form to become universal and popular, Baraka argues, it must lose some connection with the specific, original culture that gave it birth. Because the record industry figured out how to make money from them, Bessie Smith and many other blues queens were among the first African-American musicians able to preserve their art for posterity. They sang simple, vivid narratives that telegraphed whole lifetimes of experience. As Southern puts it, "The blueswomen were consummate entertainers who knew how to put over a song." So it was only natural that their music came to be beloved not just by black city women who had similar lives, or by African Americans of both sexes who'd grown up in the Delta listening to local musicianers and bluesmen, but by fans and musicians of all races everywhere.

But as blues grew more popular and universal, Baraka says, it started to become a "stylized response"—a beautiful, powerful "artifact." As performance music, it became something else entirely apart from daily life, in the same

Bessie Smith, known as the "Empress of the Blues," was one of the most famous and influential of the early twentieth-century blues singers. Her debut recording, released in 1923, sold one million copies in its first year.

way that the African slaves' religion had been severed from daily life. In Baraka's analysis, the great success of the blues queens helped take the music one step further away from its African roots.

Cordially Yours
Blind Lemon Jefferson

"Blind" Lemon Jefferson was a Delta bluesman who was among the many musicians in Mississippi who were being actively sought out by record companies in the 1920s. These musicians were usually only accompanied by a guitar or banjo, and would be recorded using field equipment or sent to a recording studio in the Northern cities.

# 6

# The Kings
# Eclipse the Queens

In the mid-1920s, a major shift took place in the "race record" business. In search of the next lucrative wave of popular music, the recording companies of the urban North sent talent scouts out through the Delta countryside to seek unknown musicians in the "downhome" or "country" blues tradition, as well as singers of spirituals and other "nigger music," as it was dismissively called. When these musicians were found, they'd either be sent North to record in a studio, or would be recorded on the spot using field equipment.

As the cultural offspring of the traveling songsters of an earlier generation, these musicians were—with extremely rare exceptions, such as "Memphis" Minnie—all men: Charley Patton, Tommy Johnson, "Mississippi" John Hurt, "Blind" Lemon Jefferson, and many others. Unlike the queens of classic blues, who were usually supported by elegant jazz combos, these men generally sang and accompanied themselves with guitar or banjo. (Another strain of piano-based instrumental blues had a parallel but separate development which will be examined in a later chapter.) On occasion they would be supported by bandmates playing some of the instruments one would typically find in the countryside among both white and black rural musicians: mandolins, crockery jugs, washboards, or kazoos.

But for the typical bluesman of this era, the essential performance involved just three implements: his voice, his guitar, and a knife or some other object to be used as a "slide" over the guitar strings. These country blues artists were recorded in droves during the late 1920s, and their huge popularity effectively ended the golden era of the female blues diva.

For lyrics, the country bluesmen—like their female counterparts in "classic" blues—used a repertoire of standard folksong ideas, reorganized and personalized to make an effective statement. As Palmer explains in *Deep Blues*, "Originality in the blues . . . is not a question of sitting down and making up songs out of thin air. Yet a blues singer whose songs consist entirely or almost entirely of borrowed phrases, lines, and verses will claim these songs as his own, and he will be right." Certain lyrical formulas came from older ballads or spirituals, or were simply folk sayings or everyday clichés. Palmer explains:

> Phrases like "I'm goin' up the country" or "you've got to reap just what you sow" were repeated by countless wandering songsters throughout the latter half of the nineteenth century and probably figured in black music before Emancipation. But while one singer might say, "I'm goin' up the country, mama, in a few more days," another would sing, "I'm goin' up the country, baby, don't you want to go," or "I'm goin' up the country where the water tastes like wine."

Some musicians were particularly adept at incorporating local or personal references into songs that were otherwise made up of this generic material. Bekker writes that Charley Patton's songs often included people he knew—"friends, enemies, police, bootleggers, foremen, growers, and the like." "Mississippi" John Hurt was so accurate and specific in his mention of rural towns, jails, and other landmarks that in the 1960s, a folklorist used the lyrics to Hurt's "Avalon, My Home Town" as a road map, and was able to find his way to the bluesman's house.

Also reflecting the black style of folksong performance that developed in the nineteenth century was the abrasive, rough, highly emotional vocal manner in which these early twentieth century artists sang. They'd use falsetto or break into full-voiced growls if the nature of the song called for such theatrics. Southern describes their unique approach:

> The melodies and harmonies were full of "bent" tones [i.e., highly colorful notes that fall between the notes on European-based scales and may seem "out of tune" to unfamiliar ears] or were strangely without tone graduations in the manner of field hollers. The men slapped their instruments, stomped their feet, and beat the strings of the guitar, producing percussive effects. And they worked out special devices—drawing the blade of a knife across the strings of the guitar as they played, or using a broken bottleneck or a brass ring or a piece of polished bone slipped over the finger—to produce whining tones reminiscent of the human voice, so that their instrument could "talk" to them.

Unlike formally trained musicians who tend to revere their instruments as sacred objects on which there are "right" and "wrong" ways to play, bluesmen treated their instruments as tools that could to be used in any way to make any kind of sound the song seemed to call for. "It was common practice to retune the strings of the guitar or banjo so that the open strings formed the notes of a chord or some other combination of tones specially favored by the bluesman," Southern writes. "The harmonica player, or harpist, imitated trains and the howling and wailing of animals; a favorite imitation was the 'fox chase.' Special effects were obtained by fluttering the fingers, cupping the hand over the instrument and open and closing them to vary the sound."

This experimental and improvisational working method—an "anything goes" sensibility that you see at the birth of a new style—quickly developed into a set of common practices or traditional gestures. Musicians passed standard performance techniques from one to the other, although the great ones each would extend and elaborate on those techniques to create a unique, individual form of expression. In a place like the Delta, where many musicians congregated in the vicinity of Dockery's plantation, the transfer of ideas and the consolidation of a standard "blues idiom" happened live and in person, with men like Charley Patton becoming teachers or mentors to other musicians. Later on, the widespread availability of blues recordings would accelerate and broaden the transfer of musical ideas—but would also help solidify certain sounds into blues clichés.

For example, compared to the relatively rigid twelve-bar format and tonic-subdominant-dominant harmonic structure of many modern blues songs, early blues tunes were often much simpler and looser in terms of both rhythmic and harmonic structure. As time went on, it would become harder and harder for a blues-oriented musician to forge a truly new, different sound or to depart from the standard structure, and still have it be called "the blues."

The first man to record on blues guitar was named Sylvester Weaver. But his "Guitar Blues" and "Guitar Rag," released in October 1923, were not as successful as the later "Lawdy, Lawdy Blues" and "Airy Man Blues" by "Papa" Charlie Jackson, released in August 1924. Jackson's recordings opened the floodgates, and within the next five years, dozens of Delta bluesmen were given recording contracts.

Paramount Records—the company that had cashed in on Mamie Smith's best-selling "Crazy Blues"—employed a number of local agents in the Delta, including a white music-store owner in Jackson, Mississippi, named Henry Spier. Spier knew Charley

Lacking money for formal instruments, resourceful musicians often learned to make music from any objects at hand—or mouth. Here, the man seated on the ground plays a homemade bass, while he and the guitarist also blow through a couple of kazoos.

Patton's music, and he recommended it to Paramount's recording directors. In 1929, the local Delta celebrity traveled to Gennett Record Studio in Richmond, Indiana, to cut his first sides: "Pony Blues" on the A-side backed with "Banty Rooster Blues." Interestingly, Paramount also simultaneously recorded some of Patton's religious music—the songs "Prayer of Death" and "I'm Going Home"—but released those under the pseudonym "Elder J. J. Hadley" to avoid turning away religious folks who wouldn't be caught dead buying a record by a blues singer. For some reason that has been lost to history, Paramount also recorded Patton on another forty-five singing two blues songs as "The Masked Marvel."

All these solo records did so well that the company later brought Charley Patton to a studio in Grafton, Wisconsin, where he played in a duo with a friend of his, a fiddle player and singer named Henry "Son" Sims. In *Deep Blues*, Palmer writes that Patton and Sims "were a good match. Sims sawed roughly at his instrument, which sounds like it may have been homemade, producing incisively rhythmic lead lines and an unsentimental, astringent timbre." The acclaimed singer-guitarist Willie Brown, one of Patton's students from the Dockery area, may have also appeared on that record as a so-called commentator, a background vocalist who sings or speaks short improvised riffs behind the main lyric (a practice similar to the kind of spontaneous "commentating" that black churchgoers often engaged in, both then and now).

By the time of his recordings, Charley Patton was showing the signs of his hardworking, hard-partying life. In poor health, he made no further recordings for Paramount after 1930, although just before his death another company invited him up to New York to record a few more sides. Patton died of heart failure in April 1934, not far from Dockery's plantation. "Not surprisingly for the time and place," Bekker writes, "his death was covered in neither the local nor national press. There is even the possibility that he had walked out on [his common-law wife] Bertha Lee in Holly Ridge in the final days of his life and died alone in Indianola." Patton's music would go on to influence many bluesmen, even those who were not in the right place and right time to have encountered him in the Delta.

Like many of the female "classic blues" queens, some of the Delta bluesmen of the late 1920s were stars in their own time, only to be almost entirely forgotten by later generations. Interestingly, though, a few who did not achieve great commercial success at the time of their original record releases were "resurrected" during the great folk revival of the 1960s. In that later time period, and again in the 1980s, musicians and historians were taking a renewed interest in "roots" music—blues and other rural styles from both white and black musicians. "Mississippi" John Hurt (1894-1966) was an excellent guitar player and witty, sophisticated songwriter. His recordings for Vocalian Records in the 1920s, although beloved by a small circle of fans, sold poorly, and his career went nowhere. Thirty-five years later, folklorist Tom Hoskins—the one who'd tracked down Hurt using his song as a map—and other revivalists rediscovered Hurt's music, and their enthusiastic attention allowed Hurt to launch an impressive concert career during the last few years of his life.

Booker T. Washington "Bukka" White (1909-1977) had a similar story. As Bekker writes, "Bukka White was a sharecropper, convict, secondhand furniture dealer, and master of the Delta blues, but his first attempt at a career in music was a complete commercial failure . . . Although White was locally revered as an enormously talented bluesman, his fame never spread much beyond the Delta before the 1960s." In 1962, both Bob Dylan and Buffy Sainte-Marie recorded versions of White's tune "Fixin' to Die." This inspired several other folk artists to search for the composer, who was still living in his hometown of Aberdeen, Mississippi, and still playing the blues. Having captured the interest of younger musicians and fans, White reemerged as a touring, recording, internationally renowned figure. "More fortunate than many of his blues-playing contemporaries," Bekker notes, "White enjoyed wide acclaim for his music before his life ended."

An old African tradition held that the guitar, banjo, and fiddle were "devil's instruments." Thus, although most African Americans acknowledged a deep, general connection between music and spiritual worship, many churchgoing blacks considered guitar-based blues to be "evil."

# 7

# Sacred
# or Profane?

**B**y the early twentieth century, black Americans had been brought wholly into the Christian church of the former slaveholders. On an explicit, conscious level, there remained no direct references to the religious practices or concepts of the African past. But the religious culture of these women and men still retained a certain deep connection to that of their ancestors—particularly when it came to the functional role of music. In *Blues People*, Baraka described the significance of this so-called "African retention":

> The Negro church . . . has always been a "church of emotion." In Africa, ritual dances and songs were integral parts of African religious observances, and the emotional frenzies that were usually concomitant with any African religious practice have been pretty well documented . . . This heritage of emotional religion was one of the strongest contributions that the African culture made to the Afro-American. . . . "Spirit possession," as

it is called in the African religions, was also intrinsic to Afro-Christianity. "Gettin' the spirit," "getting' religion," or "getting' happy" were indispensable features of the early American Negro church and, even today, of the non-middle-class and rural Negro churches. And always music was an important part . . . acting in most cases as the catalyst for those worshipers who would suddenly "feel the spirit." [As an old African saying dictated,] "The spirit will not descend without song."

But what kind of song, exactly? For many churchgoing African Americans, there had always been a distinct division between sacred music that served only to glorify God, and profane music that instead glamorized a sinful life of drinking, swearing, gambling, fornicating, and violence. That is exactly why Paramount Records decided to release bluesman Charley Patton's religious songs under a false identity: to keep from offending or scaring off blues-fearing buyers. Hymns and spirituals, in this common view, were squarely on the side of the angels; the blues were devil's music. But there was more to this dichotomy than just the contents or subject matter of the songs, as the scholar Jon Michael Spencer explains in his detailed study *Blues and Evil*:

> [C]hurch folks of the old South believed it was the devil who taught wayward Christians to play the "devil's instruments," instruments the evil one himself was thought to have played. Among early modern Britons, the "devil's instruments" included the flute, pipe, or cittern; among Africans enslaved in America and their descendants, they were the guitar, banjo, and fiddle. Black men or women who played one of these instruments were thought by some to be in actual communication with the devil and thus to be "devil's preachers."

Blues artists themselves had complicated, sometimes vexed notions about the music they were compelled to make. After all, they grew up in the same God-fearing neighborhoods and households as the folks who would sooner drop dead than set foot in a barroom where guitars were being played. Although they may have lived life in a noisy and rebellious manner, bluesmen generally held the same worldview and religious cosmology as their churchgoing relatives, friends, and neighbors.

And yet, if they found themselves utterly drawn to the blues, these musicians had to come up with ways to make sense of their passion within the terms of their community's religious worldview. If they were going to be involved in a "devilish" life, they had to justify it to themselves. There were probably as many different strategies for doing so as there were different styles of guitar-picking. But according to Spencer and other scholars, what made any of these self-justifying strategies possible was an easily overlooked fact: that although these African Americans were Christians in name and in practice, they actually did retain certain African concepts that were quite different from their European counterparts.

Thus, for example, scholars have noted that a "devil" in old African terms was actually not quite as bad a fellow as the Christian image of Satan at this time. Many have argued that, for black Americans, the word "devil" had actually come to signify the old West African god named Legba. In the pantheistic religion of the Fon people of Dahomey, Legba was not a fallen angel or an embodiment of pure evil, but something slightly more benevolent—a trickster or conjurer who could potentially be called upon for good purposes as well as bad ones. Compared to the "more somber and threatening Devil portrayed in hellfire-and-brimstone sermons," Palmer writes, Legba had a "mordant sense of humor" and he "delight[ed] in chaos and confusion." Spencer notes that in African lore, Legba "is both malevolent and benevolent, disruptive and reconciliatory, profane and sacred, and yet the predominant attitude toward him is affection rather than fear."

Spencer claims the confusion or conflation of the Christian devil with Legba is easily explained if you know that "early Christian missionaries to the Fon taught their African converts that Legba was Satan." Here in America, among enslaved Africans who had Christian cosmology imposed upon them, Legba in turn began to take on the more "satanic" qualities of this tradition.

Scholars use the term "holistic" to describe African religious cosmology. In a pantheistic, holistic worldview, "good" and "evil" are not strictly opposites as they are in Christianity, but are ingredients in a complicated reality presided over by a whole host of major and minor deities. This helps explain why Southern blacks of the late nineteenth and early twentieth century might use the words like "evil" (or "devilment," or "hell") in a relatively weak sense some of the time—to describe earthly problems such as a cheating husband or wife—but also in the strong, dualistic sense at other times. As a result of the clash between the holistic and dualistic views of the reality, scholars believe, early twentieth-century African Americans were constantly negotiating between two concepts of the devil, on an unconscious and unarticulated level. But if this is true, then perhaps the mere fact of a "less evil" image of the Devil—a trickster who used to be known as Legba—ultimately gave blues players a philosophical "ticket" that made it possible to engage in devil's music. The price for such a ticket may not have been cheap—but it didn't amount to eternal hellfire and damnation.

Eddie James "Son" House Jr. (1902-1988) was one bluesman able to reconcile his fundamentally religious nature with his musical calling by conceiving the blues as an *extension* of the pious life, not its opposite. As a musician, House was a late bloomer who, as a youth, believed that playing guitar was a sin. Yet just like Patton, House had always felt a strong calling toward music. Brought up in a strongly religious family, he sang in sacred choirs and preached in a local Baptist church. By the time he was twenty years old, he was made pastor of that church, although he lost the job after having a steamy, scandalous affair with a woman in her thirties. He lived his next few years on a rollercoaster—or perhaps the better metaphor would be "seesaw"—similar to the one Charley Patton was usually riding, as Son House alternated periods of drunken carousing and music-making with periods of sobriety and preaching.

In his late twenties he got into a drunken gunfight after a party, and shot a man dead. Although he claimed it was an act of self-defense, Son House was sentenced to the state penal farm at Parchman, Mississippi, "where he had to work at the sort of manual labor he tried to avoid by preaching and singing the blues," Palmer writes. "But he was obliging and polite when, after around two years, a judge in Clarksdale reexamined his case and gave him his freedom." (At this particular time in the South, judges treated crimes between blacks with a cavalier attitude, and disposed of such cases however they pleased. In situations where whites were victims of crimes, however, African Americans were often accused, hunted down, and lynched by popular mobs without benefit of a police investigation or jury trial, and the local judicial authorities were just as cavalier in looking the other way.)

When the judge strongly recommended that the ex-convict leave the area, House quickly took his suggestion and wandered up toward northern Mississippi to a town called Lula in the vicinity of Dockery's. It was here that he ultimately developed his own intense, haunting, memorable style of blues which combined the influences of his church-music roots with what he learned from his friend Charley Patton and other living blues legends like Rubin Lacy and James McCoy. Although his guitar technique was always rather limited, "his instrument became a congregation, responding to his gravelly exhortation with clipped, percussive bass rhythms and the ecstatic whine of the slider in the treble," Palmer writes. "There was nothing fancy about House's music, except perhaps for the rich embroideries that occasionally found their way into his singing, but it was a stark, gripping, kinetic music that demanded to be danced to and would have left few listeners unmoved."

By this time, Son House had apparently abandoned, or else learned to ignore, his childhood belief that guitarists were close kin to Satan's messengers. He had found ways to reconcile his ever-present religious yearnings with his desire to make music—a

Blues musician Jimmie Lee Robinson recording in a converted studio that was once a church. Once considered vulgar and indecent by many religious African Americans, blues music has generally come to be seen as an alternative but equally valid form of spiritual expression. Blues singer Son House, for example, sang that preaching the gospel and "preachin' the blues" were two sides of the same coin.

reconciliation that was uneasy and incomplete. In "Preachin' the Blues," the singer begins with a sarcastic jibe at the clergy— which, according to Bekker, was probably a way to justify his abandonment of preaching. In the third stanza below, House suggests that the blues have the power to drive away the spirit. But in the final verses, he seems to be saying that the blues, in fact, are another way to rouse the spirit, as equally valid as traditional gospel preaching:

Oh, I'm gon' get me religion, I'm gon' join the Baptist church
Oh, I'm gon' get me religion, I'm gon' join the Baptist church
I'm gon' be a Baptist preacher and I sure won't have to work

Oh, I'm gon' preach these blues now, and I want everybody to shout
Mmmmmm-hmmmmm, and I want everybody to shout
I'm gon' do like a prisoner, I'm gon' roll my time on out

Oh, in my room, I bowed down to pray
Oh, in my room, I bowed down to pray
Say the blues come 'long and they drove my spirit away

Oh, and I had religion, Lord, this very day
Oh, I had religion, Lord, this very day
But the womens and the whiskey, well they would not let me pray

. . . .

Oh, I got to stay on the job, I ain't got no time to lose
He-e-e-ey, I ain't got no time to lose
I swear to God I've got to preach these gospel blues
(*Spoken*: Great God Almighty!)

Oh, I'm gon' preach these blues and choose my seat and sit down
Oh, I'm gon' preach these blues now and choose my sit and sit down
When the spirit comes, sisters, I want you to jump straight up and down

In his treatise *The Spirituals and the Blues*, James H. Cone writes that when black church people condemned the blues for being vulgar and indecent, it was only because they hadn't understood them properly. "If the blues are viewed in the proper perspective," writes Cone, "it is clear that their mood is very similar to the ethos of the spirituals." Whereas religious songs spoke of the glories of the next world and of the soul's heavenly transcendence, the blues were an equally important, functional way of expressing the troubles and absurdities of this world. The blues spoke of everyday agonies that seemed like they'd never be transcended—whether they were caused by poverty:

> I stood on the corner, and I almost bust my head
> I stood on the corner, almost bust my head,
> I couldn't earn me enough money to buy me a loaf of bread

or by loneliness:

> All day long I'm worried
> All day long I'm blue
> I'm so awfully lonesome
> I doan know what to do

or by love gone wrong:

> My man left this morning, just about half past four
> My man left this morning, just about half past four
> He left a note on the pillow saying he couldn't use me now more
> I grabbed my pillow, turned over in my bed
> I grabbed my pillow, turned over in my bed
> I cried about my daddy until my cheeks turned cherry red
>
> It's awful hard to take it, it was such a bitter pill
> It's awful hard to take it, it was such a bitter pill
> If the blues don't kill me that man's meanness will.

In Cone's view, spiritual music and blues music are two sides of the same coin, and both are necessary ways of expressing the totality of black American experience in the early twentieth century. There is no opposition between them, but a symbiosis. Perhaps this is exactly what Son House was driving at—in less formal and more memorable terms—when he sang,

> Oh, I got to stay on the job, I ain't got no time to lose
> He-e-e-ey, I ain't got no time to lose
> I swear to God I've got to preach these gospel blues
> (*Spoken*: Great God Almighty!)

According to an old, familiar legend among Southern blacks, it was possible
to meet the devil at a crossroads at midnight, sell him your soul, and receive
unlimited musical talent in exchange. Huddie "Leadbelly" Ledbetter was one of
many blues musicians who actually played up the notion that he had some kind
of connection with the devil.

# 8

# At the Crossroads

While a man like Son House found ways to reconcile godliness with guitar playing and was able to "preach the blues" just as he also "preached the gospel," other musicians took a different tack: they reveled in the notion that they were playing the Devil's music and were possibly risking their eternal souls. Some of these men consciously cultivated the idea that they had met the Devil—or rather, the trickster-god Legba—at a "crossroads," and the deity had granted them supernatural musical powers. The St. Louis-born pianist and guitarist William Bunch (1905-1941), who billed himself as Peetie Wheatstraw, often referred to himself as "the Devil's Son-in-Law" or the "High Sheriff from Hell." According to Palmer, the Delta bluesman Tommy Johnson (1896-1956) seems to have decided consciously to embody the trickster's personality:

He took to carrying a large rabbit's foot around with him and displaying it often, and his performances were spectacularly acrobatic. "He'd kick the

69

guitar, flip it, turn it back on his head and be playin' it," remembers Houston Stackhouse, a bluesman who played with Johnson in the late twenties. "Then he get straddled over it like he was ridin' a mule, pick it that way. All that kind of rot. Oh, he'd tear it up, man. People loved to see that."

These men may have been consciously playing on the superstitions and religious beliefs of their more churchly neighbors in order to spice up their performances; or they may have been telegraphing their own ambivalence at living a sinful life that they'd ultimately have to pay for; or perhaps they were doing a little of both. In effecting the trickster personality, bluesmen also played into some common white stereotypes about blacks: namely, that evil lurked underneath their dark skins. In *Blues and Evil*, Spencer notes that white-dominated mainstream culture perceived the black blues singer as a "bad nigger." In 1937, when Huddie Ledbetter, better known as Leadbelly (1885-1949), received governor's pardons for two murders in Texas and Louisiana, *Life* magazine reported the event under the headline "Bad Nigger Makes Good Minstrel."

Because even law-abiding Americans have always been fascinated with criminality—witness the tendency to romanticize the outlaws of the Old West or the Italian and Irish mobsters of the mid- and late twentieth century—the "bad nigger" stereotype no doubt helped sell records to white audiences, if not at the time of their original recordings in the 1920s, then certainly during the folk revivals of the 1960s and later. (In the 1990s, the same dynamic helped fuel the huge popularity of black urban "gangsta" rap among the children of white suburbia.)

Extreme natural talent, whether in music, mathematics, or other pursuits that average people find difficult, has long been associated with notions of the supernatural. Thus it was said about many a bluesman that he could only have learned to play and sing so well if he'd met the Devil at a crossroads and sold him his soul. Of all the Delta guitarists to be trailed by such stories, Robert Johnson (1911-1938) became the most famous. Bekker writes that Johnson's intricate, sophisticated playing served as a link between the simple country blues of most Delta players and the ornate, electrified guitar blues that developed in cities such as Chicago and Memphis in the 1940s. Johnson lived a very brief and extremely transient life. "Everyone who knew him or ever saw him play would mention that his visits were brief," writes Bekker, "and his departures were hasty and mostly without ceremony." This fact helped fuel the notion that Johnson, as he sang in ones of his most masterful songs, actually did have a "hellhound" on his trail.

But the rumor of Johnson's bedevilment took hold mostly because of the revolutionary quality of his playing. According to Palmer in *Deep Blues*, in 1930, Johnson was hanging around Robinsonville, Mississippi, and trying to learn the blues from Son House and Charley Patton. At first he sounded every bit the novice he was, and when the older musicians were drunk, they frequently ridiculed him. But then, Johnson abruptly left the area.

> He returned some time later—a few months according to some accounts, but in fact probably more like a year—singing and playing with the dazzling technique and almost supernatural electricity that were so evident on his first recordings in 1936. Years later, several of Johnson's relatives told blues researcher Mack McCormick that Robert had sold his soul to the Devil and claimed they knew the exact backcountry crossroads where the deal was made. "The Devil came there," said one, "and gave Robert his talent and told him he had eight more years to live on earth." Robert probably encouraged the rumor, as Tommy Johnson had earlier.

Johnson played the guitar "in a revolutionary manner" that made him the Delta's first modern bluesman, Palmer says. "He made the instrument sound uncannily like a full band, furnishing a heavy beat with his feet, chording innovative shuffle rhythms, and picking out a high, treble-string lead with his slider, all at the same time. Fellow guitarists would watch him with unabashed, open-mouthed wonder."

Another one of talent scout Henry Spier's Delta "discoveries," Robert Johnson cut many sides for American Record Company

The late '60s rock band Cream, which featured Eric Clapton, updated Robert Johnson's "Cross Road Blues" with hard-driving, electric instrumentation for their own hit, "Crossroads."

(ARC) starting in late 1936. These recordings were immediately influential—the up-and-coming bluesman Muddy Waters learned as much as he could from them—but also had a huge impact on the development of rock music when they were reissued in the 1960s. His songs included "Terraplane Blues," "Kind Hearted Woman Blues," and the masterpiece "Cross Road Blues," which later became the basis of the hit "Crossroads" by British guitarist Eric Clapton and his band Cream. In "Cross Road Blues," Johnson himself makes use of the superstitious stories told about him:

> I went to the crossroads, fell down on my knees
> I went to the crossroads, fell down on my knees
> Asked the Lord above "Have mercy, save poor Bob, if you please."
>
> You can run, you can run, tell my friend-boy Willie Brown
> You can run, tell my friend-boy Willie Brown
> Lord, that I'm standin' at the crossroad, babe I believe I'm sinkin' down

Like many of the men living the life of the wandering blues-man, Robert Johnson was a charmer and womanizer—and his flirtatious nature would prove to be his undoing. Writes Bekker,

> Like most performers, Johnson had more than his share of "groupies." But in the Delta, a performer could quickly lose his fingers, or even his life, at the hands of a jealous boyfriend or husband, or even a drunken plantation worker seething at the comparatively easy life of bluesmen. Friends warned Robert often enough to be careful about his flirtations, advice that typically went unheeded.

One night in August 1938, Robert was playing with some other musicians at a joint called the Three Forks in Greenwood, Mississippi. By some accounts, Johnson was paying too much attention to the wife of the man who owned the bar. Bekker describes what may have been the decisive moment in Johnson's final days:

> When a half-pint of whisky with a broken seal was brought to the players, [an older musician named] Sonny Boy slapped it away, admonishing the younger man never to drink from an opened bottle. But Johnson, reckless literally to the end, disregarded Sonny Boy's advice and drank heartily from another opened bottle of liquor that arrived soon thereafter.

Johnson began retching and became delirious later that night, and although he survived whatever it was that poisoned him—probably strychnine—he was weakened. A few days later he contracted pneumonia and died, having never seen a doctor. For some who mourned him, Robert Johnson had simply been unlucky and had gone too far with his libertine ways. But others would never believe entirely in such a simple explanation. To a great many superstitious people—not just Southern blacks at the time, but white American and European fans who revered his music decades later—the hellhounds had finally caught up to Robert Johnson, and had demanded payment for his supernatural musical gifts.

Generally used for formal, written music, the piano eventually became incorporated into the blues tradition by innovative, self-taught improvisers. Three hundred years earlier in Europe, the compositions of Johann Sebastian Bach (shown here at a harpsichord, a precursor to the piano) had shown the Western world the advantages of the keyboards' "well-tempered" tuning system. But in order to mimic the different, non-standard, African-rooted tuning used by blues guitarists, twentieth-century blues pianists developed ways of striking or slipping between keys to create the appropriate sounds.

# 9

# Piano Blues

Although the blues has always been, and continues to be, a predominantly guitar-based and voice-based musical idiom, the sound and the spirit of the blues did find its way into a few piano-based styles. One of the reasons the blues worked so well on guitar is that, from the start, individual musicians made use of the instrument's capacity to be tuned at whim. That is why old country blues may sound a little weird or "out of tune" to one's ears if one is thoroughly steeped in traditional Western music.

Tuning systems vary throughout the world; the twelve-tone, "well-tempered" system of major and minor scales that we know in Europe and the Americas is not an absolute or naturally occurring set of pitches. Rather, it is an artificial, man-made division of pitches that, for various historical reasons, became popularly established as "common practice" in Europe in the Baroque era (1600-1750), largely through the work of Johann Sebastian Bach (1685-1750) and other influential composers. The indigenous music of Asia and Africa, as well as the early folk music of Europe and the Americas, used and continue to use different tuning systems or conventions.

Today, student musicians interested in rock, blues, or jazz will be schooled in something called the "blues scale." They will be told, for example, that a blues scale, in comparison to a seven-pitch major scale in the well-tempered system, usually contains a flatted third and a flatted seventh—the pitches known as "blue notes." This is merely a convenient explanation that originated when musicians trained in Western "common practice" tried to understand the unusual pitches that blues guitar players and singers tended to use, by rationalizing it or referring it back to the system they were familiar with. But in reality, "blues notes" and the "blues scale" do not correspond exactly with the flatted third and flatted seventh of the major scale. They are probably either the remnants of an African tuning system that the grandchildren and great-grandchildren of slaves still retained, or a wholly new African-American system created by the interaction of African folk music and the "common practice" European-based music of the educated white American elites. (Poor white country folk also tended to use scales other than the well-tempered in their folk music.)

The piano is more than an example of an instrument tuned according to the well-tempered system. It is in some ways the very reason why the tuning system became so popular and so entrenched in Western culture. When Bach composed his preludes and fugues in the two-volume *Well-Tempered Clavier*, it was in order to demonstrate the system's flexibility and usefulness—particularly the ease with which a musician can transpose a tune or piece of music from one "key" or "tonal center" to another. But the piano, unlike the human voice, the guitar, or many other string and wind instruments, has a limitation: there is no way to play pitches that fall "between" the notes on the keyboard.

Adapting the blues to fit the piano, then, required a musician to find ways to approximate the sound of the in-between, sometimes ambiguous "blues notes" or the non-traditional tuning system of a singer or guitarist. They did this by playing two consecutive notes (technically known as a minor second) at the same time to create a clashing, dissonant sound, or by quickly sliding a finger from one note down or up to the next note, to imitate the sound of a guitar or voice sliding between pitches.

Because the well-tempered sound wasn't suited to the original blues sounds, blues pianists probably learned to make good use of the fact that in the kinds of performance environments they enjoyed, pianos were likely to be beat up, burned by cigarette stubs, stained by beer, and horribly "out of tune" by Western common practice standards.

In the introduction to his piano technique book, *Barrelhouse and Boogie Piano*, pianist Eric Kriss writes about the honky-tonks, bars, juke joints, and barrelhouses in which pianists like Roosevelt Sykes, Peetie Wheatstraw, and Jimmy Yancey held forth on Saturday nights:

> This was the world of the blues piano player: sitting in a corner all night, pounding out stomps, low-down blues, fast boogies, drinking beer, shouting and having a whopping good time. It was a fast scene and the life expectancy wasn't too long, but thousands of men chose to leave family and job behind to follow the rough lumber camps, haunt roadside barrelhouses or drift through dusty, obscure hamlets in search of an audience.

African-American piano style owes a lot to Scott Joplin, the prolific composer and popularizer of ragtime music. Although ragtime had some African folk elements, it was a written-down music that generally required training in classical Western piano technique. Ragtime of the nineteenth century gave birth to stride piano of the twentieth century, which "tended to be a northern style" whose practitioners often had some formal musical training. Blues-piano playing, in contrast, was improvisational rather than written, and had a folk-music heritage among unschooled or self-taught musicians who'd been heavily influenced by the blues guitarists in their milieu. In his history *Black Music of the Two Worlds*, John Storm Roberts writes that the various styles of piano blues contained a high degree of "retained" African elements, particularly the lack of melody in the European sense, the use of repeated rhythmic figures (called *ostinatos*), triplets, and the heavy use of three-against-two cross-rhythms:

> This is most clearly shown by boogie-woogie, a spinoff of barrel-house blues whose basis is the repetition of short, rhythmic phrases by both hands that continually cross each other rhythmically . . . There used to be a theory that the growth of boogie-woogie was due to lack of pianistic skill on the part of self-taught musicians, who were compelled to keep their left hand in one position and to repeat the same figure constantly. This is a classic example of the absurdities that can be advanced in the attempt to avoid looking Africa in the eye. Aside from the fact that playing these ostinato basses is very far from easy, boogie-woogie is only one form of barrelhouse piano, and the other forms do not in fact use such "restricted" basses.

During the rush to record bluesmen and blueswomen in the 1920s, and before the Great Depression of 1929 forced the recording industry to abandon the "race records" market, a significant number of blues pianists were able to record—including Albert Ammons (1907-1949), Meade Lux Lewis (1905-1964), Roosevelt Sykes (1906-1983), and Clarence "Pine Top" Smith (1904-1929). Pianists like these became fixtures in both rural southern communities and urban northern ones.

Struggling to make ends meet, African Americans in all parts of the country often threw "rent parties." The hosts would charge a few dollars per person and provide food, drink, and rowdy entertainment—most often supplied by a boogie-woogie pianist. As Southern describes in *The Music of Black Americans*, these solo musicians took on the function of entire dance ensemble—in terms of volume as well as musical density. They preferred a piano that was out of tune in order to get the effects they wanted. Generally they used an old upright, from which they removed the front cover and put newspapers behind the hammers and tin on the felts. Then the pianist set to work, and the dancing began, often to last the entire night.

In 1938, a New York record producer named John Hammond— who had helped launch the careers of jazz greats Count Basie, Billie Holiday, and Benny Goodman—organized a concert called "From Spirituals to Swing," the first presentation of African-American music to be presented in New York's famed and prestigious Carnegie Hall. During the December twenty-third concert, three boogie-woogie pianists—Meade "Lux" Lewis, Albert Ammons, and Pete Johnson—played acrobatic instrumentals and also accompanied the impressive blues singer Joe Turner. It was such a sensation that the musicians were booked for an extended engagement at the Café Society Downtown. Their popularity in New York, writes Palmer in *Deep Blues*,

> helped launch a national boogie-woogie craze that lasted into the early fifties, infecting popular singers (the Andrews Sisters did "Boogie Woogie Bugle Boy"), swing bands (Tommy Dorsey had a hit with "T. D.'s Boogie Woogie"), hillbilly acts (the Delmore Brothers recorded "Hillbilly Boogie"), and of course blues musicians, who had been playing or implying boogie rhythms for decades.

In the 1940s and 1950s, these infectious rhythms also played a role in the development of early rhythm and blues (R&B), which paired blues-style singing with an accompaniment of boogie-woogie style piano and electric guitar. B. B. King, an adept traditional bluesman from the Delta who moved to Memphis rather than Chicago, was one of the most popular

Boogie-woogie piano (played here by one of its greatest practitioners, Meade "Lux" Lewis) was an almost athletic style of playing, based on repetitious but rhythmically complex phrases. Boogie-woogie was launched into popularity when Lewis and two other pianists played during the famous "From Spirituals to Swing" concert of African-American music at Carnegie Hall in 1938. The boogie sound remained a national craze until the early 1950s.

and influential artists of this genre in its heyday. As of this writing, he is still an active performer specializing in electrified blues and traditional R&B (which can be distinguished from "contemporary R&B," a label that covers a wide variety of black popular music).

The word "boogie" has an ambiguous etymology that seems to reflect the "mongrel" background of this uniquely American piano style. "Boogie" may be related to "West African words such as the Hausa 'buga' and Mandingo 'bug,'" according to Palmer, "both of which mean 'to beat' as in 'to beat a drum.'" On the other hand, "the words 'bogy,' 'booger,' and possibly 'boogie' have long been common in English slang, and have in fact been used to refer to blacks, or to dark apparitions like the bogy man." Once again, we see how difficult it is to untangle anything resembling "pure" separate strands of influence in a country where two entirely different cultures have been forced by history to accommodate one another.

Musicologist Alan Lomax made field recordings of many forms of American folk music for the Library of Congress during the middle part of the twentieth century. In the 1940s, Lomax went to Clarksdale looking for the legendary Robert Johnson but instead found Muddy Waters. Waters was less than enthusiastic about playing for Lomax, since he was hoping for a contract with one of the big Northern record companies. But after hearing for himself for the first time on Lomax's recording equipment, Waters knew he could make it as a blues musician.

# 10

# The Blues Goes Electric

The country began to recover from the Great Depression in the late 1930s, and in the 1940s the national economy received a significant boost as America entered World War II. At this time, huge numbers of African Americans migrated out of the South and rural Midwest into the urban North and the West Coast in search of decent-paying jobs and educational opportunities that were still very scarce in rural Dixie. In the Delta, a traditional style of country blues continued to thrive, especially once radio stations started broadcasting both live music programs and recordings that reached into black homes throughout the region. (In 1941, for example, station KFFA in Helena, Arkansas began featuring harmonica player Willie "Rice" Miller and guitarist Robert "Junior" Lockwood on its daily "King Biscuit Time," a program that ultimately lasted until 1981.) But in the cities, and especially in Chicago, a new style of blues was being forged.

Muddy Waters, born McKinley Morganfield (1915-1983), ultimately became the most important innovator in what came to called "urban blues." Muddy—nicknamed so because as a child he loved to splash in the wet, rich, swampy soil of the Mississippi Delta—was raised by his grandmother in Rolling Fork and later in Clarksdale. In *The Story of the Blues*, Bekker writes, "Waters had a conventional childhood for the region; he helped his grandmother with chores, worked in the cotton fields, attended church, did some preaching, and amused himself and his friends by playing Jew's harp and harmonica."

At seventeen or so, he purchased a guitar for two dollars and fifty cents from the Sears and Roebuck catalog and started learning how to play. Growing up in the thirties, Waters was one of the fortunate young musicians who could learn their craft from recordings as well as directly from the practitioners. Bekker described his influences:

> He listened to phonograph records of the leading musical figures of the day, local and regional players such as Blind Lemon Jefferson, Memphis Minnie, LeRoy Carr, and Lonnie Johnson. He also heard the sophisticated urban jazz and blues performers. But it was the Delta guitar work of Robert Johnson he admired the most. Waters was also deeply impressed by the vocal intensity and fierceness of Johnson's mentor, Son House.

In his twenties, he worked as a tractor driver for twenty-two and a half cents an hour at the Stovall Plantation, supplementing his meager wages by establishing a juke house where he served his own moonshine whiskey. In 1941, two folk-song collectors from the Library of Congress, Alan Lomax and John Work, came poking around Clarksdale in search of Robert Johnson. They were too late, as Johnson had already died. But the locals referred them to Muddy, who was playing guitar in a country string band, and who was said to play a lot like Johnson. When Lomax and Work found him, Muddy was less than enthusiastic about their project. After all, he was hoping to be recorded by one of the big Northern music producers that would put his music on a forty-five. But Muddy agreed to the folklorists' fee of ten dollars per song, and sat down with his steel-bodied guitar and bottleneck slide. He sang a tune he called "Country Blues," which began:

> It's gettin' late on in the evenin' child, I feel like, like blowin' my horn
> I woke up this mornin', found my, my little baby gone

In *Deep Blues*, Palmer imaginatively recreates the scene that must have followed when Lomax played back the aluminum disc recording:

> He put down the guitar. It was a hot, quiet Saturday afternoon; most of Stovall's hundreds of blacks were off in Clarksdale, shopping and mingling with blacks from neighboring plantations, and there wasn't any traffic on the winding dirt road outside the house. Muddy sat listening to the stillness for a few moments and then he heard those first glancing guitar notes and his rich, booming voice playing back, boldly lifelike, on Lomax's machine. The first thing he thought was that he sounded as good as anybody's records. "I can *do* it," he said to himself. "I can *do* it."

Two years later, Muddy moved to Chicago. His first priority was to find a good job. But then it was time for the tall, vigorous twenty-eight-year-old to meet the local musicians—which wasn't too difficult as soon as he started playing local house parties and other low-paying gigs—and to figure out how to make his mark.

Chicago at the time was a fertile garden of an almost mind-boggling variety of music, especially jazz and blues. By the mid-1930s, according to Bekker, urban jazz had expanded far from its New Orleans roots to become "a quirky amalgamation of pop, folk, and classical music." Sophisticated swing music was all the rage, and all over the country, both black and white musicians—usually, but not always in segregated bands—earned their livelihood playing for ballrooms full of dancers. Meanwhile two virtuosos, trumpeter Dizzy Gillespie and alto saxophonist Charlie Parker, were about to give birth to "bebop," a fast, furious, complex form of modern jazz that would define the "common practice" approach for jazz musicians for the next several generations, into the present day.

Compared to these bold innovators, a man like Muddy Waters represented a more conservative approach within the African-American musical tradition. Palmer opines that if an inquisitive, progressive musician like Robert Johnson had lived long enough to make his way North, he "would probably have perfected an electric, jazz-influenced brand of modern blues." Muddy, in contrast, "stayed with the old, richly ornamented, pentatonic blues melodies that still sounded much like field hollers and the spine-chilling bottleneck guitar figures and chopping bass runs he'd synthesized from local sources, primarily Son House and Charley Patton."

Muddy got his first electric guitar in 1944—a gift from an uncle living in Chicago. Soon thereafter he got his first "big break" when he got a fifty-dollars-a-week job playing with the house band at a South Side club called The Flame. The pianist for the band was Sunnyland Slim (1907-1995), a fellow Mississippian who was very well-connected in Chicago's music production circles. With Slim and bass player Big Crawford, Waters made his first recordings for Chess Records. At a session in 1946, the band played two sides that featured Sunnyland and two that featured Muddy. According to Bekker, Muddy's career was off to a less-than-inspiring start:

> In later years Muddy and [Chess Records owner] Leonard Chess would form a close and trusting relationship, but at the outset of their association, Chess evidently didn't think much of the big Mississippian. He hesitated for several months before releasing Muddy's two tracks, and even then didn't promote them.

Like many in the music industry, Leonard Chess was accustomed to the slick, sophisticated, and jazz-oriented "jump" blues and smooth classic blues they'd been hearing from artists such as Louis

Muddy Waters and his bandmates moved beyond the Delta tradition to forge a new style of electrified blues known as "urban" or "Chicago" blues. Chicago blues recordings on the Chess Records label became hugely influential among rock 'n' roll bands, particularly the "British invasion" acts of the 1960s.

Jordan and Nat "King" Cole. But when Muddy—along with his bandmates, including the legendary Little Walter on harmonica—brought this raw, straight-ahead, "primitive" Delta sound to Chicago's clubs, the crowds went wild. Bekker describes it as "a driving, macho sound with an evil edge that appealed to both sexes."

By the early 50s, Chess had been brought around somewhat, and his company released a string of recordings, including "Rollin' Stone," "She Moves Me," and "Long Distance Call."

These songs defined the sound of Chicago blues and made stars out of Muddy Waters and Little Walter, as well as a man named Willie Dixon, a bassist and gifted songwriter whose tunes "I'm Your Hoochie Coochie Man" and "I'm Ready" became phenomenal vocal hits for Muddy.

In these years, Muddy transformed himself from a talented musician into a powerful performer who traded on his personal magnetism and air of fierce sexuality (a transformation that won adulation from many people but also criticism from those who felt he was playing directly into white stereotypes of the "oversexed" black male). Willie Dixon's songs, in particular, created for Waters a marketable image as "the bedroom root doctor, the seer-stud with down-home *power* and urban cool," according to Palmer. But he never lost touch with the gritty Delta music that formed him. Palmer writes that even as his music became more rhythmic and his performance style more flamboyant and his lyrics flashier, Waters "kept playing his unmistakable slide guitar and singing his old Delta favorites."

As it rose to national prominence, Muddy Waters' band, known as the Headhunters, became a revolving door of great and up-and-coming musicians. Little Walter left in 1952 to form his own band, although he continued to record occasionally with Waters. Many of the other musicians who apprenticed in the Headhunters—Elmore James, Otis Spann, Junior Wells, Luther Johnson, Earl Hooker—went on to become blues legends in their own right.

More than any other single blues artist, Muddy Waters sowed the seeds of modern, electric-guitar-based rock and roll. It began with a 1958 appearance of the Headhunters in England, which, according to Bekker,

> electrified audiences, and developments there in the aftermath no doubt greatly affected more than a few of the budding musicians who would soon lead the "British Invasion" of the United States during the 1960s. When it came, the invasion featured a lot of the music written by Muddy, his peers, and his forebears.

But the universal appeal of this distinctly African-American music was also what ensured its eventual banishment to the margins rather than the mainstream of popular music. As they raided the archives of the great innovators of Delta blues and other black music, these young, white rock musicians may have felt nothing but respect and admiration for men like Robert Johnson or Muddy Waters. But that respect and admiration could not prevent the ascendance of rock and roll from nearly killing off its own roots.

After nearly a century in which most black Americans lived in a kind of legal, political, and economic limbo—neither slaves nor fully empowered citizens—the individuals and organizations involved in the Civil Rights Movement of the 1950s and 1960s made significant strides in the fight against segregation and institutionalized discrimination. Although historians typically consider the movement to have begun with Rosa Parks and the Montgomery bus boycott in 1955 and to have ended with the passage of the Voting Rights Act in 1965, people still debate today whether the work of the movement is truly ended. But in that tumultuous mid-century period, the highly visible struggle for black equality spilled over into other forms of rebellion and revolution among white people, particularly the young men and women who chose to reject the traditional values of their families and live lives outside the mainstream. The beatniks and yippies of the 1950s and the hippies and flower children of the 1960s were, in some large measure, taking their cultural and political cues from African-American freedom fighters.

Young white musicians and their fans rejected the smooth, highly orchestrated, often desexualized pop their parents enjoyed and looked to the great storehouse of African-American folk music for inspiration and rebellious wisdom. Blues musicians had repeatedly said that the music they played was "the only medium through which they could articulate their inner feelings," writes Ellison, and that it was "a lifeline through years of repression." Many mainstream white youths, feeling boxed in by the conformist values and routine emotional repression of their parents' generation,

Elvis Presley sang music based in the blues and boogie-woogie traditions and became immensely popular with white audiences in a way few black artists had.

believed they could relate. Their translations and transformations of downhome blues led to the birth of rock and roll.

A half-century later, the rock and roll "revolution" has become almost completely co-opted by the mainstream: television advertising regularly uses classic blues-based rock to lend a rebellious individualist sheen to products that are actually mass-produced and thoroughly mainstream: cars, beer, and so on. But at its birth in the 1950s and 1960s, rock music truly was subversive, particularly in its openness about sexuality. Indeed, the term "rock and roll," as many commentators have pointed out, was originally a euphemism for sex.

Elvis Presley, Jerry Lee Lewis, Buddy Holly, and Bill Haley and the Comets were among the artists of this era to achieve national and international prominence as whites performing a fundamentally black musical sound grounded in boogie-woogie and blues. At the same time, a few rare black artists were successfully marketed to white record buyers—for example, Chubby Checker, who had a hit in 1960 with "The Twist."

Then came the Beatles. The legendary four lads from Liverpool—a very large, cosmopolitan seaport in England where they would have heard plenty of Nashville country music and Mississippi blues in local pubs—worked magic with their resourceful, imaginative fusion of downhome blues, urban blues, rock and roll, country music, folk music, and even classical influences. They were an immediate success in America, particularly among young women, who came to every stateside Beatles appearance in hordes and surrendered themselves in a frenzy of screaming, crying, and fainting. The palpable sexual element and profound emotionality of these events was not unnoticed by contemporary commentators. Ellison quotes Eldridge Cleaver, a writer and the leader of the radical Black Panther Party during the late 1960s and early 1970s, who had more than a few words to say about the Fab Four:

> The Beatles were on the scene, injecting Negritude by the ton into whites, in the post-Elvis Presley-beatnik era of ferment . . . Rhythm and Blues . . . is the basic ingredient, the core, of the gaudy, cacophonous hymns with which the Beatles of Liverpool drive their hordes of ultra feminine fans into catatonia and hysteria for Beatles fans, having been alienated from their own bodies so long and so deeply, the effect of these potent, erotic rhythms is electric. Into this music, the Negro projected—as it were, *drained off,* as pus from a sore—a powerful

sensuality, his pain and lust, his love and hate, his ambition and despair. The Negro projected into his music his very body. The Beatles, the four longhaired lads from Liverpool, are offering up as their gift the Negro body, and in so doing establish a rhythmic communication between the listener's own Mind and Body.

But the Beatles also sanitized the blues to a great extent, and made its sexual power a bit safer for sheltered middle-class white youths by couching it in terms of love and romance. Soon after the Beatles' arrival, Mick Jagger and the Rolling Stones would work to strip away that safe exterior by revisiting the downhome roots of the music. As Ellison notes, the Stones' "smash hit song *Satisfaction* used blues words and a rock sound; it exemplified the talent they had for bringing out the latent malignity of the blues, for their aggression was not inhibited by the racial pressures constraining the original black artists."

Spurred by the British invasion, "[m]ore and more white American musicians began to listen to the blues and absorb the black sounds," Ellison writes. "Multiple white blues bands sprang up just as they had in England. The music they produced ranged widely from the only slightly transformed blues of the Paul Butterfield Blues Band and the Lovin' Spoonful to the dramatically different fulminations of . . . The Doors." Meanwhile, folk singers of the era who were grounded in a tradition of social protest—particularly Bob Dylan and Woody Guthrie—made their own transformations of the blues and other black folk music, this time focusing less on the sexual aspects and more on the political dimensions.

As rock became the dominant type of pop music in the 1960s, many of its most successful artists tracked down their Delta blues or Chicago blues heroes, and their attention sometimes led to broader fame and fortune for black musicians who'd been operating mostly within the African-American community. Muddy Waters, for example, had grown a bit embittered by the late 1950s as young blacks seemed to lose interest in his style of blues and

The Rolling Stones were among several English bands to find inspiration in American blues music. Approaching their music in a more raw and aggressive way than the Beatles, the Rolling Stones helped make white audiences aware of the authentic African-American roots of rock and roll. Muddy Waters later credited the Stones for bringing about a revival of his own music in the 1960s.

demonstrated a preference for newer forms of soul and R&B. He later credited the Rolling Stones for bringing his music to white audiences for the first time and sparking a major revival in his career in the 1960s.

Yet the huge commercial success of rock also struck some black musicians as painfully, bitterly ironic. The huge success of international stars like the Beatles or Bob Dylan helped consolidate the music industry into a giant capitalist juggernaut, making it much harder for smaller labels, local clubs, and local or regional radio stations to survive. With fewer places to be heard and to build an audience, musicians playing styles other than mainstream rock were destined to be marginalized. In many parts of the country, white radio programmers, record producers, and listeners still balked at what their parents' generation would have called "nigger music"—but happily embraced the wealth to be made by marketing white performers playing fundamentally black music. Thus, among many African-American musicians and critics, rock and roll's "reverence" for its black musical antecedents was a form of exploitation, and nothing more.

The ramifications of these issues belong properly to the history of rock music, so we do not have the time or space to explore them here at length. But it is interesting to note that, in our own time, similar debates crop up again. Today, rap or hip-hop music has eclipsed rock as the best-selling form of popular music. Millions of white suburban youths have embraced this essentially black creation. Yet it is not unusual to hear the Beastie Boys or Eminem, white rap artists, played on predominantly white, "alternative rock" stations that would never play a black rapper—or on the other side, to hear black artists dismissing or ignoring such musicians entirely, treating them as musical thieves and frauds. In America, even as our music refuses to be segregated, our culture and our minds remain stubbornly divided in many ways.

There is still a small but loyal audience for traditional, electrified, guitar-based blues. At annual blues festivals throughout the country (especially in Chicago, Memphis, Detroit, and various towns in and around the Mississippi Delta), one may find octogenarian Delta bluesmen playing alongside young college-educated black musicians from Boston, former sharecroppers sharing stages with blues bands from Europe or Japan, and young white women hollering the blues with enough class and conviction to make Bessie Smith nod her head appreciatively.

Although most Americans listen to country/western, rap, or rock in one of its many traditional and contemporary flavors, there are still dozens of radio stations around the country—mostly small, public, local ones—that offer blues programming once a week or so. The giant music superstores of today all keep at least a small selection of blues CDs on hand. So the resources are available, if one is curious.

Some of today's blues have taken on a museum-like quality: if it hews too closely to the songs and performance styles of another era, the music can seem stuck in the past. And if Imamu Amiri Baraka's analysis from the 1960s was on target, perhaps the blues has been severed from its functional African roots and there is no way for the music to be as authentic and meaningful as it once was.

Yet for some young artists, who approach fifty-year-old techniques and concepts in a fresh, personal way, the blues is still a living tradition, a source of inspiration that helps them articulate their individuality. Perhaps, if one finds himself bored by the latest posturing of multimillionaire "gangstas" or the insipid, over-produced, mass-marketed sounds of the latest female teen idol or boy band, one might find himself drawn to the simple yet powerful charm of the blues—the granddaddy of all American music.

| | |
|---|---|
| **1619** | First arrival of Africans in the English colonies at Jamestown, Virginia. |
| **1661** | First of the so-called Black Codes legally recognizing slavery are established. |
| **1780–1790** | Slavery gradually abolished in Pennsylvania, Massachusetts, other New England states, and the Northwest Territories. |
| **1807** | U.S. Congress abolishes the slave trade. |
| **1843** | The Virginia Minstrels organize the first white minstrel show in New York City. |
| **1861–1865** | The Civil War takes place. |
| **1863** | Abraham Lincoln issues the Emancipation Proclamation. |
| **1865** | Congress enacts the Thirteenth Amendment to the U.S. Constitution, abolishing slavery. |
| **1865** | First permanent black minstrel troupes are established. |
| **1890** | "Jim Crow" laws are enacted in the South. |
| **1901** | Black theater singers Bert Williams and George Walker make the first known recording of black musicians. |
| **1903** | W. C. Handy hears blues slide guitar played in a Mississippi train station. |
| **1913** | First black theater circuit is established, leading to the foundation of the Theater Owners' Booking Agency (TOBA). |
| **1920** | Mamie Smith's "Crazy Blues" launches the "race record" industry. |
| **1938** | John Hammond produces the black music survey concert, "From Spirituals to Swing," at Carnegie Hall in New York City. |
| **1954** | The U.S. Supreme Court overturns legal segregation of schools in the South. |
| **1955–1965** | The Civil Rights Movement takes place. |
| **1962** | Willie Dixon and "Memphis Slim" Peter Chatman found the American Folk Blues Festival. |
| **1964** | U.S. Congress enacts the Civil Rights Act. The same year, the Beatles and the Rolling Stones first tour the United States. |
| **1968** | Muddy Waters releases his album *Electric Mud.* |
| **1990** | A two-CD collection of Robert Johnson recordings is released, selling over one million units. |

Baraka, Imamu Amiri [Leroi Jones]. *Blues People: Negro Music in White America.* New York: William Morrow & Company, 1983.

Bekker, Jr., Peter O. E. *The Story of the Blues.* New York, Friedman/Fairfax Publishers, 1997.

Cone, James H. *The Spirituals and the Blues: An Interpretation.* Maryknoll, NY: Orbis Books, 1991.

Ellison, Mary. *Extensions of the Blues.* New York: Riverrun Press, 1989.

Harrison, Daphne Duval. *Black Pearls: Blues Queens of the 1920s.* New Brunswick and London: Rutgers, the State University, 1988.

Kriss, Eric. *Barrelhouse and Boogie Piano.* New York: Oak Publications, 1973.

McNeill, William H. *Keeping Together in Time: Dance and Drill in Human History.* Cambridge, MA: Harvard University Press, 1995.

Palmer, Robert. *Deep Blues: A Musical and Cultural History, from the Mississippi Delta to Chicago's South Side to the World.* Reprint Edition. New York, Viking Press, 1995.

Roberts, John Storm. *Black Music of the Two Worlds: African, Caribbean, Latin, and African-American Traditions.* 2nd ed. New York: Schirmer Books, 1998.

Southern, Eileen. *The Music of Black Americans: A History.* 3rd ed. New York: W. W. Norton & Company, 1997.

Spencer, Jon Michael. *Blues and Evil.* Knoxville, TN: University of Tennessee Press, 1993.

Baraka, Imamu Amiri [Leroi Jones]. *Blues People: Negro Music in White America.* New York: William Morrow & Company, 1983.

Bekker, Jr., Peter O. E. *The Story of the Blues.* New York, Friedman/Fairfax Publishers, 1997.

Palmer, Robert. *Deep Blues: A Musical and Cultural History, from the Mississippi Delta to Chicago's South Side to the World.* Reprint Edition. New York, Viking Press, 1995.

**http://www.fred.net/turtle/blues.shtml**
[That Blues Music Page]

**http://www.theprimer.co.uk/**
[The Rhythm and Blues Music Primer]

**http://www.island.net/~blues/**
[BluesWEB]

## ABOUT THE AUTHOR

**Sandy Asirvatham,** a graduate of Columbia University with a B.A. in philosophy and economics and a M.F.A. in writing, is a freelance writer and jazz pianist/singer living in Baltimore. As a fan of jazz and rock, she found that researching and writing this book deepened her appreciation for the blues roots of these and all other popular American musical styles. Her other books for Chelsea House include a history of the police in America and an examination of the late seventeenth-century Salem witch trials.